Split Second Selling

ACHIEVING WINNING RESULTS IN THE SALES GAME

Drew Stevens, PhD

For Christine, my love, my soul mate, my forever.
And for Andrew and Ashley; throughout your wins and losses,
I am always proud to be your father.

Cover Design: Douglas Peters
Interior Design & Production: EFG Publishing. Inc.; www.efgpublishing.com

TRADEMARKS: Split Second Selling™, Split Second Customer Service™, and
P.R.A.C.T.I.C.E.™ are trademarks of Drew Stevens.

FIRST EDITION
ISBN: 0-9788755-9-1

11   10   09   08   07   5   4   3   2   1

Published and distributed to the trade by:
Golda Publishing
St. Louis, Missouri
www.gettingtothefinishline.com

What's Inside?

What's Inside?

Message from the Coach

Years before I got into selling, I was an adolescent living with a dysfunctional family. I was seeking love and attention amidst constant fighting and disrespect. I needed an outlet.

■ *Soaring Over Life's Hurdles*

My outlet was track and field. I entered the sport late in my middle school years with no training and little natural talent. But I had one thing that set me apart—determination and passion.

I wanted to succeed in this new-found sport that I loved. I practiced three to four hours a day, partly as an escape from a cold home, but also in a quest to excel at the sport.

Without knowing how powerful it would be, I began to write down my goals and objectives. My first goals were simple things such as, "I want to finish a race." Then it was "win a race." Then it was "become the team captain" and finally, "set some school records." In just three years, I became the captain, the most valuable team member, and set five school records; three of which were in hurdles. I finally found something that enabled me to create, to embody happiness, and to feel like a winner.

For many years, my determination on the track continued to work for me in business. I was a successful sales professional and then a successful sales manager. Then years later and within a six month period, I was tested again. I was terminated from three jobs and lost my mother-in-law to cancer. Following these events, I lost touch with my importance, my happiness, and more importantly my passion.

■ *Getting Back on Track*

I changed my mind in a *Split Second*. I questioned what made me happy, what made me whole, and what made me create. The answer was simple—selling.

I used the same methods and skills I learned from creating success in track and field to create my business, Getting to the Finish Line. I set goals, I clearly see my mission, and I never lose touch with my passion.

Today I successfully tour the world helping others maximize their selling effectiveness. I help others not only sell but create, love, and prosper. While some think of me as a selling coach, I consider myself a personal coach. One who wants to help you find your passion, align your energies, and seek your fortune.

■ *How to Use Split Second Selling*

This book is written with the pretense that the concepts and theories taken separately can assist in making split-second decisions to create change. My desire is to help you find one thing that you can use to make rapid change in your selling career.

Split Second Selling is organized into four parts: practice techniques, game day strategies, tips for coaches and managers, and motivation to cross the finish line. It is designed for you to read in short bursts to get the specific information you need at the moment. You can read just the sections that you need, or you can read it cover to cover.

Recall for a moment the movie from approximately 1990, entitled *City Slickers*, starring Billy Crystal. In this movie Mr. Crystal's character is seeking the meaning of life and the meaning of his happiness. The quasi-villainous character in the movie, played by Jack Palance, indicates to Mr. Crystal that happiness is about one thing—"Just one thing."

When Mr. Palance is questioned about what this one thing is, he states he does not have an answer. The reason, he states so clearly, is that the one thing is up to the individual. Each person in life gets to choose one item that enables him or her to obtain the fulfillment they seek.

■ *Into the Starting Blocks*

This book is about your journey in finding that one thing. It took me almost 20 years to find it and I am happier now than I have ever been. This book is about achievement. This book will not create immediate answers to selling issues but will help you to make split-second decisions to enhance your selling skills and make needed changes so that you become more productive.

The most difficult part for any new endeavor is to begin. If you want change, you must get to the starting line. If you want results, you must get to the starting line. If you put into action your new desires along with the changes you must make, these split-second decisions send you sprinting to the Finish Line!

May God bless you in your journey,

P.S. I tripped over more hurdles than I can remember on my way to those school records. Have faith in yourself, pick yourself up when you fall, and keep your eye on the Finish Line. Turn the page to take your first step off of the starting line...

Part I:

Come to P.R.A.C.T.I.C.E.

chapter 1

Going Pro in Sales

What is the oldest profession in human history? Many will be surprised to learn that it is selling. The art, the passion, and the history of sales began during biblical times. It was during the growth of our world that individuals began to exchange goods and services for money. Although sales professionals were called something different during these times, they were very respected people in their communities.

Sales professionals bartered for services. They traveled hundreds of miles and months on end to have someone purchase their goods and services, and they took pride in what they did.

Selling today is not much different from what it was 2000 years ago. However, selling today is a very competitive and fast-paced business that takes time, courage, an ability to relate well to people and, moreover, an ability to ride a roller coaster.

■ Why Sell?

Why not? One of the most versatile professions and the most interesting profession in the world is that of sales. Nothing—and I mean nothing— happens to any firm, any organization, or any business without sales. Selling for any firm is where it all begins. Selling turns on the lights, selling pays the salaries, selling helps with research and development —selling helps everything! There is not one portion of a firm that is not affected in some way by sales.

Many do not understand this: Selling is the beginning for any company. Sales must take place for a company to maintain its ability to supply customers with products and maintain visibility in the marketplace.

Unfortunately, sales professionals tend to get stereotyped into "sleazy" unconcerned individuals who want nothing more than to line their pockets with cash. This stereotyping has been particularly hard to shake for certain industries and companies.

Whether you are an established sales professional or a new member of the field, you should be very proud of your profession.

There is nothing that provides me with more pleasure, more purpose, and more passion than helping a prospective client satisfy their wants and needs.

If you think about the world of professional selling, you not only resolve pressing issues but you also get to help people meet challenges and ease pain. You are a physician, a consultant, a trusted friend trying to help another undergo a transformation so as to assist with present business and personal issues and make their lives easier.

For more than 25 years I have sold products and services from Main Street to Wall Street. I can tell you nothing has satisfied me more than knowing that I have assisted thousands of people during my tenure as a sales professional.

■ *The New Sales Professional*

The core of professional selling in business and practice has not changed too much in the last 2000 years. Selling is still about matching a buyer with a professional who is interested in a particular product or service. What have changed are the methods and practices in which to communicate to potential and prospective buyers.

As of the writing of this book, we live in an age where business seems to be accomplished at the speed of sound. The internet, cell phones, fax machines, email, voicemail, and a myriad of other devices are not only accessible to much of the world but also essential. As a result, sales professionals seem to conduct business 24 hours a day, seven days a week, 365 days a year.

Given the world of the internet and delivery of information at the speed of light, clients feel the need to communicate wherever, however, and whenever they need it.

Today's sales professionals find an increasing challenge to meet that need. A sales professional today is armed much like a security person or handyman, with a box of tools and trinkets that denote his or her trade. Cell phone, pager, laptop, WiFi and other modern channels of communication assist the selling professional in remaining connected all day.

However, much to the chagrin of many sales professionals, what separates the good sales professional from the great is an uncanny ability to create, maintain, and build relationships. Even with all of the electronic means of communication at the their disposal, clients still want and need a relationship with sales professionals. Most importantly, many clients need someone they can trust and count on for many years to come. After 25 years in a completely different market, I still maintain many of my original client relations.

Salespeople are like trusted friends and confidants. Don't get me wrong—I'm not telling you to become a therapist or a counselor, but I do suggest that the further you can befriend a client and assist them with meeting the challenges they face, the more trust you will build. Also, the more you resolve issues and offer suggestions for future work, the better your relationship and the more you will sell.

If you take only one suggestion from this book, make it this: do not sell for money, do not sell for prestige, and do not sell to satisfy your desire for material things. Sell because you love it. Sell because you enjoy resolving client issues and because you enjoy a challenge.

■ Five P's of Successful Sales

When I conduct my sales seminars, I offer the keys to sales success. You are receiving them here for the first time in print. After a review of my own self-development over 25 years of successfully selling products, I have concluded that the art of selling comes down to five very special and very important terms.

They are:

- Preparation
- Planning
- Purpose
- Passion
- Persistence

In consulting and leading a myriad of sales forces over the years, I have found the preceding five traits to be essential characteristics of all successful sales professionals. Even the failed fictional salesman, Willie Loman, of Arthur Miller's play "Death of a Salesman," had passion and persistence. In order to achieve, you too must have those characteristics —and more!

■ *Preparation*

The most important part of any sales professional's job is to prepare for each and every sales call. The successful sales professional will always know who he or she is calling, as well as why they are calling and how they will sell the product or service.

A sales professional is much like a general on the battlefield, an athletic coach at a game, or a chess player at a tournament: always thinking ahead, strategizing to determine their next move. You might say a sales professional is like a nurse in an elementary school before the fall and winter seasons hit. The nurse knows that students will get ill from the spread of germs, so she conveys information about how to avoid getting sick to the students prior to the start of flu and cold season. Salespeople do the same.

Successful salespeople are always prepared. They understand the client, the industry, the company, and the specific pain the client is dealing with. Prepared sales professionals also know how to get information should there be a question that stumps them. Put simply, sales professionals are problem solvers much like a physician trying to understand the reason for an illness. Sales professionals know how to ask the correct questions to understand the issue and move immediately to problem identification and resolution. It should be a very rare occasion when a prepared sales professional does not know where to turn to get an answer.

■ *Planning*

Planning is one of the most important parts of sales preparation. From answering a telephone to making a call to understanding the client and the industry, planning is the single most important part of selling. If you do not know who you are speaking to and what you will say, then how can you have a conversation?

Selling without planning is much like going on a blind date. You do know that the person is male or female and that they want to meet you and communicate with you, but that is all. You cannot be a problem solver if you do not understand to whom you are speaking and how you can meet their needs.

There are several low-cost or no-cost planning resources that are musts for sales professionals because they can take you from good to great in a short time. They are the annual report, news, and company and industry information.

■ *Annual Report*

This important multisection document is a must-read. The first few pages contain a letter from the company's president or CEO that outlines new products, reports on growth and operational woes, and describes plans for maintaining their competitive edge. This initial section indicates how you and your producers can help the company.

Also of importance is the listing of company officers and board members. Review the list to see if your contact is in the upper tier and to identify board members who could be future customers. Finally, read the financial report and review the numbers so that you understand the company's financial position. From this section you determine if the company can afford your product; or perhaps you can identify areas in which you can help them save money.

So where can you get an annual report? Call the company's department of investor relations or corporate communications, or get in touch with your contact. The latter will appreciate that you are going the extra mile to learn about the company. You may also be able to obtain an annual report from the company's web site or through a subscription-based internet service, such as *Hoovers.com* or *Dow Jones News Retrieval.*

■ *Business News*

Not enough sales professionals read *The Wall Street Journal, The New York Times*, or other national periodicals.

To properly service your customers, you must understand their successes, recognize their trials and tribulations, and help them cope with competition and the pressures of the marketplace.

Reading a major periodical will inform you about customer news and keep you abreast of business changes. Not enough time to read through the newspapers? Then subscribe to the periodicals' e-mail bulletin services for real-time updates. And although your time is limited, you should commit 30 minutes each day to reading your local newspaper's business section from front to back. Some of the online new sources I highly recommend are *www.cnn.com, www.nytimes.com* and *www. wsj.com.*. These are only my personal suggestions—you may have your favorites depending on your regional, national, and international location. However, I do suggest you subscribe to an online or off-line periodical to better understand company and industry issues.

■ *Industry News*

As important as breaking business news is, you must clearly understand the industry you service. Therefore, it is your job to follow industry news. Perhaps you are servicing a niche industry, such as Wall Street technology firms. Ask your clients and contacts about the periodicals they read to follow industry trends. You can then determine which publications are most reliable and subscribe. The payment you make for the delivery of this information is an investment in your career.

If it is difficult to locate business or industry periodicals, check the voluminous resources available online, such as *www.factiva.com, interactive.wsj.com* and *www.nytimes.com.* Also, numerous Internet portals including Alta Vista, Yahoo, and Google provide real-time business content. Review these sites to gain quick and timely information.

Certainly in today's fast-paced, information-crazed environment, there is little time to access increasing amounts of information.

However, clients want sales professionals who understand their business and competitive concerns and can use that knowledge to help them.

Clients want trust, service, and relationships. Take the time to learn their business, and your efforts will be rewarded.

■ *Purpose*

Never call a client without a purpose. You must have an intention for each and every conversation, call, proposal, and action you take. Not to say that all is calculated, but you must have a reason for why you are doing what you are doing.

Purpose helps you to answer three vtial and dynamic questions:

- ■ Who is the client?
- ■ What do they need?
- ■ Why me?

Your ability to reply to these questions will assist you with understanding what you bring to the table and how you can help the client replace their current pain with the pleasure provided by your services.

Your purpose gives you direction, like a compass that helps you to drive to your destination in the least amount of time.

■ *Passion*

I knew when I graduated from college many years ago that I wanted to do something where I helped people resolve problems. I wanted to work with people in a communication role, and I knew I needed to surround myself with people all day long. I looked at public relations, coaching, counseling, and, ultimately, sales.

After 25 years, nothing makes me happier, nothing keeps me going, nothing touches my heart more than the ability to work with and help people.

I love selling, and I am not afraid to admit it. I love the challenge of trying to meet people's needs, and I love helping people resolve their issues. I love selling.

You also need to love selling. You need to love what you do and how you do it. You need to eat, sleep, drink, and talk selling—it must be in your blood! The secret to successful sales professionals is that they absolutely, unequivocally love what they do.

Successful sales professionals love challenges, are exceptional in overcoming adversity, and love the product or service that they represent. They are never shy or reserved, and you can sense their spirit and their passion when they speak. In fact, I heard a South African phrase recently: *Enbutu,* meaning from the spirit. Successful sales professionals have an aura of spirit, of love, of passion, of commitment in everything and anything that they do. The more you can create enbutu in your sales presentations and your sales day, the more helpful you can be to your client.

■ *Persistence*

Lastly, successful sales professionals are persistent. They love, need, and yearn for a challenge. Successful sales professionals never say quit or uncle, and they never stop answering questions, resolving issues, and finding customers.

Successful sales professionals are constantly seeking new business and looking for ways to find new clients. It is the successful sales professional who is always looking for answers and finding ways to resolve client issues.

Additionally, sales professionals that succeed never take "no" for an answer. Those with the power of determination are not stubborn but are capable of seeking the needle in a haystack with such dogged persistence that they stand head and shoulders above anyone else. The successful sales person is someone who is still willing to go the distance even when fatigued or stumped; creating value, vision, and viability for the prospective client who is yearning for a resolution.

Every sale has five basic obstacles:
no need, no money, no hurry, no desire, no trust.

—Zig Ziglar, American Sales Trainer,
Author, Motivational Speaker

SELLING SCORECARD

List three ideas from this chapter that you will put into immediate use to begin obtaining the results you seek.

☐ *Idea:*

_____

_____

_____

Start Date: _____

Finish Line Date: _____

☐ *Idea:*

_____

_____

_____

Start Date: _____

Finish Line Date: _____

☐ *Idea:*

_____

_____

_____

Start Date: _____

Finish Line Date: _____

EVENT:

TURNING PRO

chapter 2

P-R-A-C-T-I-C-E
Selling

Welcome to the world of professional selling, a world often compared to a ride on an emotional roller coaster. One moment you are at the top of the game; the next you are plunging through an abysmal low. These gyrations are created by the effects of speaking, cajoling, and influencing individuals throughout the day.

One might think of a sales professional as a psychologist, perhaps even a psychic. Why? Many times you are trying to define the details of the relationship between yourself and a prospective client. There are also times when you are trying to anticipate the thoughts, questions, and ideas of the other party. Last, your mission is to convince them to buy based on the information they supply to you.

■ The Starting Line—Motivation

Selling is simply an emotional experience for both you and the prospective client. However, let's focus on the client to make a point. Buyers make purchases based on emotion. You have touched them physically and mentally, and they are ready to use the product or service. Your client will make a purchase because they are excited about the prospects of using this item and how it will help them. You are motivating them to make a decision.

The motivation stems from the concepts of pain and pleasure. The prospective buyer presumably is undergoing pain and requires pleasure from your product or service. This pain typically is not associated with actual physical sources of discomfort, but more commonly stems from mental perceptions of pain. Perhaps productivity or efficiency is down and the prospect seeks better methods of conducting his or her business. No matter the issue, your job is to play detective and uncover it.

Why? Sometimes clients know the reason and will tell you what they are seeking. Oftentimes, though, they do not know and you need to help them uncover the issue. The way you uncover the issue is to understand what the buyer's wants and needs are. This is actually the beginning of the selling process.

The key here is to understand whether the buyer *wants* it or *needs* it and to uncover the buyer's motivation. This is called the "Starting Line," or the "Sales Information Step." During this step, you gather information and analyze the client to best understand his or her primary interest.

■ Wants, Needs & Motives

This interest is something that the customer either wants or needs. Typically we might make mistakes by assuming that prospects want or need our service. We could assume that a person needs a car for work; however, we might discover that they can also take the bus. Therefore, the client might want a car but may not necessarily need it. Or we might need oil, but we might not want it! It is your mission to determine the nature of the primary interest—want or need?

Once we consider whether the prospect wants or needs our services, we then must determine the *Dominant Buying Motive*. The Dominant Buying Motive denotes why the buyer wants or needs the service. A prospective client may have either professional or personal motives that drive his or her desire for a particular service.

For example, your buyer might consider a top-tier training company to conduct sales training—a search for service that is motivated by professional interest. Another professional motive may be to bolster his professional image in his manager's eyes. In searching for a service provider to fulfill his needs, in this example, your buyer might consider a top-tier training firm that requires relatively little preparation, thereby decreasing administrative costs and loss of employee productivity. Finding such a firm certainly would fulfill the buyer's need for training and also address his motive of looking good to management.

While the buyer's motive of catching management's eye may be primarily professional, there is also an element of personal motivation. Understanding the psychology of your buyer will help you identify the fact that he is a people-pleaser who wants to be liked. Making a good purchase will not only serve his professional interests but will gain him kudos, which will feed his ego—another powerful motivator.

Although there are thousands of reasons why buyers make a purchase decision, the most compelling motive ultimately will move the buyer from mere consideration to action. The Dominant Buying Motive is that most compelling reason.

■ Building Trust

Once you understand the Dominant Buying Motive, it is necessary to persuade the client to buy. As a selling professional, you may hit a crossroad. It is at this juncture that you must clearly establish a relationship with the purchaser. It is quite simple: they need to trust you. Clients purchase from people they like and they trust.

That statement is so essential that I want to repeat it once again to emphasize its importance: clients purchase from people they like and they trust. It is vital that you begin to establish a relationship with this prospective buyer. People want honest information about what your product or service can do for them. People do not buy services or products, they buy the benefits of those services or products integrated with the relationship they have with you.

Imagine a very flat piece of land. On that piece of property is a fence; on one side of the fence is the buyer, and on the other side is the seller. On the seller side the plants that grow are called rapport, interest, motivation, and commitment. The buyer's side contains rejection, indifference, skepticism, procrastination, and fear. What you have are different attitudes and feelings from opposing sides. Your job is to build a bridge of trust, allowing you to override the indifference and rejection that selling brings.

There are several ways to understand the wants and the needs of the client. While there is a process that will be discussed further in this chapter, here are some simple steps to help prepare you.

■ Dominant Buying Motive

In the space below list a Dominant Buying Motive for your prospective Client.

Dominant Buying Motive:

_____

_____

_____

Research your client—Conduct as much research as possible so you can see what the client sees—or perhaps does not see.

Ask the gatekeeper—When you call the gatekeeper, the goal is to build rapport. Befriending the gatekeeper may help you determine how to uncover the client's Dominant Buying Motive.

Interview others—Begin to question those around the client so you can understand the pain and pleasures they have.

Research the industry—Look for the trends and the volatility in the industry. Acting as a problem solver rather than a sales professional will enable you to uncover unforeseen concerns.

Ask the client—Your use of probing questions will enable you to determine the issues. Specific and open-ended questions will help. You might also consider the use of "critical thinking" and "feeling" questions.

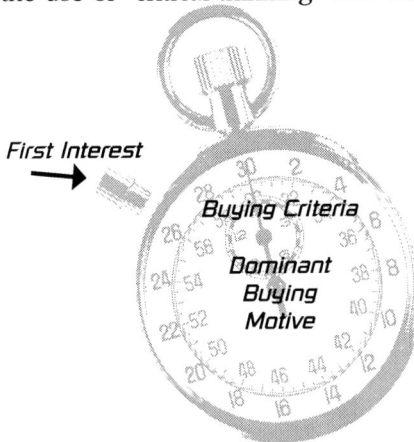

First Interest

Buying Criteria

Dominant Buying Motive

▪ *Unique Selling Feature*

Finally, there is one final step that you need to take once you start to identify what the client's wants and needs are. It is your simple mission, your selling destiny, and your road map to sales success:

> *Your mission is to identify your unique selling feature that offers a competitive advantage or benefit to your client that sets your product or service head and shoulders above anyone else.*

You cannot talk about your competitor, nor should you speak of other services. Your job is to focus on you and on your firm. It is imperative that you focus on the client's needs and how the unique features offered by your company's product or service can meet their needs.

Remember, the client wants to trust you and needs to trust you to make the purchase, so focus on what you can do for them! Keep in mind that clients aren't focused on you or your firm—they care about themselves!

Imagine for a moment that each of your clients has a set of antennas. Each of these antennas is tuned into one radio station during the sales call: WII-FM, 111.1 FM. You may not have heard of it, but everyone uses it! The radio station plays every second of every day in every mind in the world: What's in it for me radio. All me, all the time, and totally commercial free!

All your clients truly care about is what your product or service will do for them. In fact, their mental radios can only tune in the following stations:

WII-FM *What's in it for me?*

MMFG-AM *Make me feel good about myself.*

HCIB-FM *How can I benefit for myself?*

SSI-AM *Show some interest addressing me.*

GMB-FM *Give me benefits for me.*

ITOI-FM *Is this of interest for me?*

Now that you have the mindset of a successful sales professional, you are ready to enter the sales arena. As with many professions, your education and your background are the keys to your success.

For athletes, practicing and repetition are the keys to their success. The selling profession is a cross between business and athletics. To help integrate these two , you must PRACTICE selling! To get Finish Line results and higher commissions, you must PRACTICE every day! And similar to the athlete, repetition is the key to success.

■ P-R-A-C-T-I-C-E™—A Seven Step Formula for Success

Planning—The most vital process for any successful sales professional. Planning is about information gathering and research. Sales professionals must plan each call and be prepared to offer prospective clients all the essential information.

Rapport—Building rapport is one of the largest hurdles for any salesperson. You have to get to know strangers. This is the part of the sales business that most closely resembles riding a roller coaster: some people will be happy to see you, propelling you to emotional highs, while others will treat you like dirt, plunging you into emotional lows. This will challenge you daily. However, you must always be smiling and discover new ways to connect with people and help them resolve their issues.

Attention—The ability for two strangers to establish a rapport suffers greatly from technology. Buyers today are distracted by email, voicemail, the internet, remote controls, cell phones, etc. Sales professionals must rise above the din to be heard. And, more importantly, you must keep the buyer's interest in spite of the multiple distractions that are clamoring for their attention.

Conviction—This is the tool that you need to convince your client to buy from you. Sales professionals typically carry an arsenal of information for sales calls. However, each call must be customized with the tools and techniques that can truly reach the buyer. Items such as testimonials, statistical studies, charts, graphs, and schematics are just some of the items you will need.

Time Management—Many sales professionals ignore Time Management. The only way to determine if you are managing your time effectively is to understand where your daily focus is. Many sales professionals do not track interruptions or set priorities and this is what makes for a harried, unproductive day.

Interest—If you want someone to buy something from you, it is necessary that you interest them. This means using tools like rapport-building and fact-finding to determine if there is alignment between the prospect's interest and the benefits provided by your services. Remember, prospects do not buy a product, they buy the benefits provided by the product.

Close—Never forget to ask for what you came to obtain. Closing is one of the most vital steps in the sales process. If you do not close, you do not make any money. To remember when to close, use the ABC rule: *Always Be Closing.*

Evaluation—Selling is a unique business. Sales professionals constantly educate their prospective buyers with new innovations, new features, and new information. Selling is synonymous with teaching. You are always illustrating new ways your client can use your product or service for their own benefit. To do this, you must be enthusiastic about your product or service. You want to love what you do and what you sell. Your interest, or lack thereof, will illustrate itself during every presentation. And your enthusiasm must reign, even though you will get much rejection in the sales game. Finally, enlightenment comes with each and every call. Sales professionals can learn something with every call or presentation. Always have an open mind and be learning and you will gain much.

The remainder of this book will discuss further the various aspects of **P-R-A-C-T-I-C-E**™. The book will analyze each component and illustrate techniques to use daily. By practicing each aspect, you will develop new strengths and overcome the obstacles in your path.

Whether you are new to sales or have been selling for years, P-R-A-C-T-I-C-E will make you better. But you must P-R-A-C-T-I-C-E every day. There will always be hurdles to overcome, but success can be achieved with P-R-A-C-T-I-C-E.

My accomplishments are:		Rating My Skills from 1 – 9 (1 being the lowest)	Prioritize where I need assistance now!
P	Planning		
R	Rapport		
A	Attention		
C	Convincing		
T	Time Management		
I	Interest		
C	Close		
E	Evaluation		

*"It's the repetition of affirmations that leads to belief.
And once that belief becomes a deep conviction,
things begin to happen."*

—Muhammad Ali

SELLING SCORECARD

List three ideas from this chapter that you will put into immediate use to begin obtaining the results you seek.

☐ **Idea:**

_____

_____

_____

Start Date: _____

Finish Line Date: _____

☐ **Idea:**

_____

_____

_____

Start Date: _____

Finish Line Date: _____

☐ **Idea:**

_____

_____

_____

Start Date: _____

Finish Line Date: _____

EVENT:

PRACTICE

chapter 3

P-R-A-C-T-I-C-E
Planning

Salespeople need to begin someplace. During my seminars, I interview the audience to determine how sales managers ask their sales professionals to research clients. I often find that sales managers do not ask their sales team to conduct research and engage in call preparation.

I recently spoke with a client, Rick, who is a sales director with a multinational publishing company. He, too, was very surprised that his sales professionals do not thoroughly prepare for sales calls. In fact, he finds that in his industry there is a serious lack of call preparation.

Call preparation—both for *pre-selling* and for *in-process selling* is vital. Salespeople must know who they are speaking to and what they will speak to them about. More importantly, they need to know how their product or service fits with the needs of the client.

There are two methods available for sales call planning: personal and professional.

■ Personal

I mentioned earlier that selling is similar to riding a roller coaster: one moment you are up in the air and the next you are in the abyss. Selling is a volatile business that requires a strong mind, body, and spirit to succeed. During my many years of corporate experience, many of my sales teams did little to prepare for the workday. They simply "rolled into the office" and began their day.

Selling is a unique profession. Your preparations should be put together with the same energy and attention to detail that a lawyer would use when preparing to speak to a client; or a doctor when preparing to see a patient; or an athlete in preparing for an athletic event. You must prepare with a purpose, with pride, and with passion.

Here are some useful tools to aid in your preparation.

■ *Goals*

Goals are the keys to your success. With goals you will accomplish more than you ever have in your entire life. Goals are nothing more than your desires, your hopes, your dreams, and your aspirations placed within a time frame. And goals are yours alone—no one can make them for you, and no one can take them away.

Goals will help you answer three vital questions for your life:

■ Who are you?

■ Where are you going?

■ How will you get there?

Goals must use the tool known as *SMART.* SMART, covered in detail on pages 72 to 75, is a process to help make your goals achievable in a short time frame. SMART will help you maintain focus, maintain the pace, and expedite your results so that you more rapidly attain success.

The SMART tool helps you remain focused. Think of SMART as a tunnel: at one end is you and at the other end is the goal. From time to time, you might bounce off the walls trying to reach your destination or even stop from fatigue. But no matter what, at the end of the tunnel is the light—your goal. The ability to know and see the goal in front of you helps you remain focused, determined, and accountable to yourself as you strive to reach your dreams.

You cannot operate your sales day without proper goals. You must have a plan for your success, know who you are going to call, and why you want to call them. Goals enable you to have a purpose so that your sales day is not haphazard. Goals let you to remain focused so that the daily distractions cannot divert you.

■ *Self-Talk*

Self-Talk is a meditative technique to help you overcome negative issues that affect your day. It is the inner dialogue that we have with ourselves to help us overcome certain limiting beliefs. You might want to call a very important client or meet with the chief executive officer of a large multinational corporation. Self-Talk can aid you in overcoming your doubt about making the call by instilling powerful phrases that you repeat to yourself.

Some examples of Self-Talk include:

■ I am powerful and can make this call.

■ There is nothing to fear about this person: they need my service.

■ I am the best sales professional, and I am on the top of my game.

■ I am a professional and can endure positive and negative circumstances. I learn from all experiences.

Self-Talk helps you achieve success throughout all phases of your life and is not solely meant for sales. All areas of your life can benefit from this remarkable method to help create affirmations and overcome negative experiences. You may even incorporate visualization with Self Talk to help broaden and enhance the experience.

■ *Visualization*

Visualization is a very powerful technique. It requires finding a very quiet space to selectively block out all interferences and concentrate on an issue that you want to see.

Visualization is like meditating with pictures. You need to visit a very quiet, dark place like a bedroom or a room with low lighting so that you can thoroughly relax. You might have music in the background to help you relax.

As you begin to forget about daily stressors, use Self Talk to become positive about things around you. And use deep breathing to slow down your heart rate and relax. Begin to imagine a place that makes you very happy. The location can be a park, the beach, the woods, a room, whatever. Picture yourself there.

When you are thoroughly relaxed, begin to visualize one positive outcome you desire. Visualize the signing of an agreement with a client or getting through to a gatekeeper. Visualize your sales success! Visualization takes time to learn and master, but once you do it you will be glad you did.

I still remember the first time I tried Visualization: I was thinking about breaking the intermediate hurdles record at my high school. I visualized my uniform, my pre-race warm up, my stretching, my competitors, where the race would take place, and the type of day. Two years to the day later, I not only won my race but also shattered the school record by doing everything I imagined during Visualization.

■ Time Management

Salespeople must prioritize their day to ensure they are not distracted from their most important goals. One can easily be distracted by customer service, payment issues, or even call reluctance. The ability to remain focused on your goals and uninhibited by such concerns is paramount to your success.

Use a daily planner to track your appointments and to help prioritize your to-do list. Plan your appointments: the number of appointments and their length. Successful salespeople are driven by planning. They understand proper planning so that time is used efficiently. In your time-sensitive environment, a keen ability to manage time will not only save you dollars, it will also help you earn them more effectively.

■ Daily Dollars

For more than 25 years I have used a daily goals sheet to remain focused. I want to understand where I want to go and how I intend to get there. I operate my business day with a laser-like focus to ensure I do not get distracted.

It is hard to argue against the idea that sales professionals are driven by the almighty dollar. Well, then it is the almighty dollar that I use to help drive my success. I simply take the amount of money that I want to make each year. I then divide the number by 220 (number of possible working days), take the result and place this on my daily goals sheet.

For example, if my annual income goal is $165,500, I divide 165,500 by 220. The result is 752. This means that I have to sell $752 of product every day to meet my goal.

Many people I know focus on the gross income they want to make each year. In a salaried position, you get what you contract for. Sales professionals obtain income based on the number of sales and a percentage of the sales in commission. Many firms do not place a ceiling on the amount of earned income; therefore, as a salesperson you get to set the upper limit for your income.

While it is nice to dream, in order to make what you want, you need to break it down in simple, attainable pieces, so it is feasible to acquire. Sound familiar? It should—it is like goal setting. Take the amount of income you want to make and break it down daily, weekly, and monthly; this prepares you to focus on customers, accounts, and issues, where you can maximize your dollars while becoming the CEO of your territory.

■ Research, Research, Research & Professional Preparation

Now that we have examined some of the personal issues to help you prepare for selling, it is time to work on professional concerns. Professional preparation begins with understanding who will buy your service and why. What kinds of accounts will you look for to buy your service, and how will you get to speak to the decision-makers?

To that end, it is imperative that you become a top-notch business researcher. The tools available today, such as the internet and other electronic sources of information, enable sales professionals to obtain data on clients wherever, whenever, and however they need. You will need many tools to enable you to understand prospective customer issues, industry trends, and client pain. You must research the implicit and explicit issues facing the client and determine how your product or service stifles their pain with pleasure.

There are three information sources that are musts for sales professionals: regional and national newspapers, industry-specific news sources, and a database to retain pertinent information.

We covered these information sources in some detail in our introductory section on the sales profession (see pages 15 to 17).

Here a few additional sources of information pertinent to the task of company research.

One of the best ways to build databases of contacts is to lease or purchase a list of contacts. There are several online databases available and each is a worthy investment. They include:

- *www.hoovers.com*
- *www.factiva.com*
- *www.leadershipdirectories.com*
- *www.dnb.com*
- *www.onesource.com*

Daily News and Information:

- *www.businessweek.com*
- *www.fortune.com*
- *www.nytimes.com*
- *www.wsj.com*
- *www.theglobeandmail.com*
- *www.reuters.com*
- *www.cnn.com*

Industry News and Information:

- *www.ebsco.com*
- *www.edgar.gov*

> *"I have yet to be in a game where luck was involved. Well-prepared players make plays. I have yet to be in a game where the most prepared team didn't win."*
> —Urban Meyer

Once you locate the company and the industry, it is necessary for you to understand who you will contact and why. While such a list might seem elementary for some, it is necessary to understand the people you contact and identify their roles. Become familiar with who they are and what they do. This will help you understand your prospects and gather the data you need to close the sale.

The process will take some effort. You will be conducting extensive analysis through thorough questioning. From time to time the research will tire and bore you, but the more you know the better and easier the sale!

■ Gatekeeper

A person who controls entry to the decision-maker is known as the gatekeeper. They often deter sales professionals from interrupting the decision-maker's day. Their role is to keep you out! You must identify this person and build a relationship with him or her. Think of the cliché, "It's not what you know but who you know." Your initial and perhaps continued success will depend on how well you establish this relationship.

You need to discover what the gatekeepers like and do not like. You might ask about movies, television shows, sports, birthdays, or favorite holidays. The more you ask, the more you know. And the more you know, the stronger the relationship.

■ Decision-Maker

This is the person who makes the final buying decision. This person can also fill one of the other roles in this list. Realize, however, that this person does not write a check, he or she only makes the decision. Moreover, he or she may not be the one who signs the contract.

■ Coach

The coach is the most important contact in your account. These people will be especially useful if the account is a complex organization and you are responsible for selling services across the company. The coach will be the one you go to for information that is "not ready for public viewing." And the coach will tell you who the main decision-makers are. Coaches are critical to your success, since they will guide you through situations that you could not navigate by means of other information sources.

■ *The Influencer*

This is the second-most important person in the decision tree. The role of the influencer is to suggest the product or service and, most importantly, the vendor (i.e., you!) to the decision-maker. This role is typically played by a single- or multi-person team given the responsibility of developing requests for proposals and requests for information. One note worthy of mention: these individuals usually have preexisting biases for particular vendors, products, and services based on prior experience.

■ *The Recommender*

The recommender is the final player in the decision tree who provides sales influence to the decision-maker. The recommender will do nothing more than recommend products and services, with or without bias. The recommender does not have decision-making power but can persuade a decision-maker.

■ *Check Writer*

Finally, there is the person who will write the check to conclude the transaction. You also must know this person. Since you will be making final preparations and negotiations with this person, it is best to understand who they are and when they will enter the purchasing process.

Although the roles here seem separate and distinct, they can overlap. For example, those of you selling to sole proprietors will find that there is no recommender or influencer other than the person with whom you are dealing. And your coach might also be a recommender or an influencer. So be on the lookout and understand who plays what role before you begin the selling process. Moreover, be prepared and get the results you seek!

If you want others to be happy, practice compassion.
If you want to be happy, practice compassion.
—The Dalai Lama

Download a FREE Copy of Drew's Sales Planning Guide at:
www.gettingtothefinishline.com/splitsecondselling.htm

PLANNING

The following questions and statements will assist you in trying to a game plan and a path to selling to new and existing accounts.

Account Name: _____ Date: _____

Primary Contact: _____ Title: _____

Type of Business: _____

Objective of the Call: _____
_____

What are my prospects goals? _____
_____

How can I help my prospect? _____
_____

What information must I know about my prospect?
_____
_____
_____

INFLUENCERS	**RECOMMENDERS**
Name: _____	Name: _____
Title: _____	Title: _____
Name: _____	Name: _____
Title: _____	Title: _____
Name: _____	Name: _____
Title: _____	Title: _____

Perceived Needs of the Prospective Client:

PERSONAL	**BUSINESS**
1. _____	1. _____
2. _____	2. _____
3. _____	3. _____
4. _____	4. _____

Needs and Benefits that I need to develop

1. _____

2. _____

3. _____

4. _____

Questions to ask to assist in developing the needs.

1. _____

2. _____

3. _____

4. _____

My Company's Strengths and Features that need to be mentioned.

1. _____

2. _____

3. _____

4. _____

Anticipated Objections and Responses:

OBJECTIONS	RESPONSES
1. _____	1. _____
2. _____	2. _____
3. _____	3. _____
4. _____	4. _____
5. _____	5. _____
6. _____	6. _____

Features and Benefits:

FEATURES	BENEFITS
1. _____	1. _____
2. _____	2. _____
3. _____	3. _____
4. _____	4. _____
5. _____	5. _____
6. _____	6. _____

What are the next steps for this account?

_____

_____

_____

SELLING SCORECARD

List three ideas from this chapter that you will put into immediate use to begin obtaining the results you seek.

☐ *Idea:*

_____

_____

_____

Start Date: _____

Finish Line Date: _____

☐ *Idea:*

_____

_____

_____

Start Date: _____

Finish Line Date: _____

☐ *Idea:*

_____

_____

_____

Start Date: _____

Finish Line Date: _____

EVENT:

PLANNING

chapter 4

P-R-A-C-T-I-C-E
Rapport

The sales profession is similar to other businesses in that we are interested in the art of persuasion. Persuasion is how we act, what we say, the words we use, and the body language we convey to convince others that we are trustworthy. Persuasion is not one thing, it is a combination of thoughts and ideas. Since the subject of persuasion is so dense, I will focus on one level of persuasion that assists the selling professional: rapport.

Rapport is a phenomenon produced through unconscious human interaction. You might say rapport is a communication tool that assists in "making connections" with the other party.

Rapport helps make effective communication work. It is not dependent upon instantly liking someone, but instead on building confidence in their competence. Rapport leads to trust.

There are several levels of rapport:

Accepting—In the rapport-building process, accepting is similar to meeting someone at a cocktail party. You are in the same room and tend to notice each other. However, instead of making an actual connection, you simply admire dress, body language, and other characteristics from afar. There is no real connection here.

Neutral—This level of rapport is very similar to accepting; however, you begin to detemine whether you would want to engage in conversation if formally introduced.

Lukewarm—You and the other party are introduced and through "small talk" sense more agreement than disagreement on issues. You are friendly towards each other.

Understanding—At this stage, both parties have similar concerns, and much agreement exists between both.

Empathetic—Not only is there agreement, you also see "eye-to-eye" on important concerns. In fact, there is so much similarity that you and the other person begin to feel that you know one another well.

Warm—Now the connection is very strong between both parties. There is mutual understanding and caring.

Hot—Caring and empathy exist to a point where emotional intimacy may be involved.

■ *How Do Sales Professionals Gain Rapport?*

This depends on the client and the circumstances, but prospect knowledge questions are one good way to build rapport. Recall that during the neutral stage, neither party knows much about the other. However, as they get to know each other, they build rapport.

This is true in selling. We must get to know the potential buyer. And there is no better way to build rapport than by asking questions.

Some of the questions that you can ask to build rapport include:

- What is your name?
- How long have you been with the organization?
- How and why did you become employed at this company?
- What is your educational background?
- What types of problems does your company have that could be solved with a particular product or service?
- What are your wants and needs?
- Are you in a position to purchase?
- How are buying decisions made in your company?
- What is the best time to contact you?

You may not want to ask these questions exactly as they are worded above, but by obtaining this type of information, you begin to create a relationship that can develop into rapport.

One of my all-time favorite books on the topic of rapport-building is *How to Win Friends and Influence People,* by Dale Carnegie.

According to Carnegie's classic text, you must:

- Become genuinely interested in other people.
- Smile.
- Remember that a person's name is to that person the sweetest and most important sound in any language.
- Be a good listener. Encourage others to talk about themselves.
- Talk in terms of the other person's interests.
- Make the other person feel important—and do it sincerely.

Finally, ensure you are actively listening to all the answers provided by the other person. Both spoken and unspoken communication are critical to successful rapport-building, and people can usually tell if you're not really paying attention to them. Good eye contact is critical.

Write down the insights you gain into your prospective buyer's issues and concerns. No matter how good your memory, you might let something slip away that could otherwise be permanently captured via good note-taking skills. You can use these facts to help build your future sales presentation.

You may feel that the importance of getting the order takes precedence over building rapport. Not true! Many salespeople ignore this step because they are overexuberant, lazy, or do not know how to establish rapport. I assure you that if you first take the time to build rapport, you will discover very interesting things and improve your chances of a successful sale. Consider the following points:

Having information reduces mistakes. The knowledge you obtain through the rapport-building process can save you time, energy, and the cost of an unsuccessful sales pitch.

Building rapport helps you understand the purchase process within the prospect's company, thus reducing the chances that you will have to call everyone in the organization to sell your product, potentially generating resentment. One objective of the rapport-building process is to use your client as a coach and advocate.

Great rapport and relationship-building creates an edge over your competitors. As you are striving to build relationships, so are your competitors. But people only continue to engage in the relationship-building process with those whom they trust and respect.

■ *Personality Power*

Rapport is a tool to enhance communication between parties. Yet there also is a wonderful tool available to you that many do not know about or use. This tool has been around for thousands of years. I first discovered it during a sales training seminar in 1984 and have never forgotten it. This tool is "personality typing" or "categorization."

One of the many imperative facets of selling is trying to understand how your selling personality is perceived by your client. More importantly as you seek new clients, you need to quickly establish rapport. However, this is easier said than done. Why? Because based on speech, body language, and vocal tone we do not always get along with others the first, and sometimes the second, time we meet them.

One of the most effective rapport tools that I use is a personality assessment known as DiSC™.

In today's competitive marketplace, success in selling is more challenging and requires a higher level of skill. Selling professionals need to gain a competitive edge, quickly! A DiSC assessment provides computer generated reports that give the sales professional a broad understanding of his/her natural sales style.

The DiSC software analyzes the personality of the sales professional and indicates their typical interactions with others. These include, but are not limited to, feelings, perceptions, body language, office setup, work style, and ethical and professional aspirations. Because all people are unique, no two reports are alike.

The understanding of DiSC helps sales professionals understand their strengths and limitations in a sales environment. This understanding can assist with tension on competitive situations, customer service, and quota attainment.

Another benefit to understanding DiSC is that a selling professional can approach a client and understand the similarities and differences to better reach client needs. Understanding DiSC styles enables a selling professional to adapt their communication style to build the trust needed to gain commitment for the sale.

Typically in business, sales professionals concentrate on the "What's in it for me" attitude. Selling situations are contradictions: the sales professional is worried about commission and the customer wants to save money. Understanding personality types allows a salesperson to quickly adapt to a buyer's behavior and linguistic style. This closes the understanding gaps that exist in sales conversations. By blending your personality to that of your client and visa versa, conversations become more productive.

I have personally used DiSC™ for over 25 years and it has been extremely helpful in creating and building relationships. I have learned to communicate more effectively by blending my conversation and body language to the personality and behavior of the other party. I credit much of my personal selling success to this assessment.

■ What is DiSC™?

People of science have been trying to understand human behavior for millenia. For instance, Hippocrates, an early philosopher, believed that climate and terrain affected human behavior and appearance.

In more recent history, Carl Jung published a journal, "Psychological Types," in 1921. He identified four personality types and reported that they create human behavior.

Jung's approach to personality assumes that there are three pairs of functions that are expressed differently in each person: extroversion-introversion; perception-intuition; and thinking-feeling. His work forms the basis of the Myers-Briggs Type Indicator, one of the first scientific tools used for categorizing personality and behavior.

Finally, in 1928, William Marston published "The Emotions of Normal People." In this text, Marston describes a primary theory still in use today to identify behavioral characteristics.

Marston's theories and personality assessments are widely used by business, education, and government agencies. The assessments have been administered to more than 30 million people worldwide. In addition to being accurate and valid, these assessments are cost-effective and easy to administer and interpret.

According to Marston, people's four primary emotional responses are:

Dominance—How people respond to problems or challenges

Influence—How people sway others to their point of view

Steadiness—How people respond to the pace of the environment

Conscientiousness—How people respond to rules and procedures set by others

These four emotional responses are referred to as DiSC™ behavioral styles. People are a combination of these four styles, although one or two styles usually predominate.

All these scientists from previous eras knew that understanding behavioral styles helps us relate to individuals. Remembering this today, we should employ various tools to help us understand our client's personality type and associated behavior patterns.

Many of us grew up with the idea that we are to treat others as we want to be treated. However, in business many people have only one primary standard: to get as much from each encounter as they can in order to better their own situation.

Understanding your prospective client's self-interest helps you build rapport and improve communication by focusing on their desires and finding ways to help them get what they want. When we focus complete attention on the client, communication becomes easier and barriers quickly disappear.

Behavioral research suggests that the most effective people are those who understand themselves and those around them. This understanding of personal strengths and possible limitations, along with the ability to identify and understand the strengths and weaknesses of others, allows one to develop strategies to meet the demands of the environment. In addition, understanding strengths and limitations closes communication gaps that can lead to dissatisfaction, complaints, and legal action.

Let's return for a moment to Marston's DiSC assessment. As mentioned above, most people exhibit a combination of DiSC traits. Pure behavioral styles are found in only a small percentage of the population:

Dominance—2 percent

Influence—less than 1 percent

Steadiness—less than 1 percent

Conscientiousness—1 percent

Yet most people have one or more DiSC traits that are more pronounced than the others. By understanding a person's predominant DiSC characteristics, you can begin to make sense of his or her professional behavior, which often influences the sales process. Below are some behaviors common to the associated DiSC categories:

Dominance

- Impatience
- Self-confidence
- Desires change; can make decisions based on very few facts
- Fears being taken advantage of
- Needs direct answers

Influence

- Emotional
- People-oriented; persuasive; often has great ideas
- Disorganized
- Fears loss of social approval
- Optimistic; can make decisions based on whether something simply sounds good

Steadiness

- Loyal; team player; good listener; patient
- Family oriented
- Possessive
- Fears loss of security
- Slow to change; bases decision on trust in others or on specific information

Conscientiousness

- Perfectionist
- Sensitive
- Accurately bases decisions on information, including pros and cons
- Fears criticism
- Needs many explanations; slow to change

While it is helpful and easy to understand the four dominant DiSC styles, Marston's work also describes the personalities by observation. Understanding your own and those of your colleagues, clients, peers, family members, etc., provides a basis for creating clear communications and understanding how each person responds to others.

When Marston studied personality he observed that people behave along two axes with their actions tending to be either extroverted or introverted. This depended on the person's perception of desiring an environment aligned with people/relationships or policy/procedure. By placing the axes at right angles, four quadrants are formed with each quadrant illustrating a specific behavioral pattern. They follow:

Dominance—Developer/Results-Oriented/Inspirational/Creative

Influence—Promotor/Persuader/Counselor/Appraiser

Steadiness—Specialist/Achiever/Agent/Investigator

Conscientiousness—Objective Thinker/Perfectionist/Practitioner

■ So Why Study DiSC?

DiSC is the number one personality assessment tool in the world today. It helps us understand our own and others' behavior, communication styles, and language. Many professionals worldwide use DiSC profiles to better understand clients and build rapport. By understanding DiSC, you will be able to identify strengths and limitations in yourself and others.

"If a man does not make new acquaintances as he advances through life, he will soon find himself left alone. A man, sir, should keep his friendship in a constant repair."
—Samuel Johnson

To obtain further information about DiSC and how it can assist your selling career or, as a FREE BONUS for buying this book, you can obtain a FREE DiSC sales assessment. Visit: *www.winningsalesassessment.com*

and mention code *Split Second Selling.*

SELF Style	Goals	Fears	High Intensity	Moderate Intensity	Low Intensity
D	Results, Control	Losing control of the environment, being taken advantage of	Direct, forceful and decisive	Competitive and self-reliant	Cautious, mild, modest
i	Recognition, Attention	Rejection and loss of approval	Enthusiastic, Sociable	Poised, confident, reflective	Controlled, pessimistic, withdrawn
S	Security, Stability	Sudden change and losing security	Patient, Predictable, Cooperative	Deliberate, Mobile	Critical, Restless
C	Accuracy, Order	Criticism and performance, lack of standards	Accurate, Conscientious	Analytical, Evasive, Persistent	Arbitrary, Defiant, Tactless

When you speak to clients, are you using the DiSC profile to define your client profile? ❑ yes   ❑ no

Journal a success story with the use of the DiSC-profile. What occurred? How did you use the DiSC to break down communication barriers to reach consensus and Win Win?

_____

_____

_____

Consider a recent conversation for the following:

When interacting with someone what questions can you ask to confirm his or her personal style and organizational issues?

_____

_____

What was the comfort level between the two of you?

_____

_____

51

What can you change next time?

_____

_____

What are some likely concerns and how can you reduce them?

_____

_____

What ongoing approach is likely to be effective when dealing with a particular style?

_____

_____

Did you obtain shared commitment? How can you achieve this?

_____

_____

What follow-up expectations are likely with that person?

_____

_____

How does this style need to be serviced by you in the future?

_____

_____

What achieved, productive results can you build on to expand your communication with them?

_____

_____

How can you improve contact with a client?

_____

_____

Reference: Bonnstetter, B. (1984). The universal language of DiSC. 10th ed. Scottsdale, AZ: Target Training International.

SELLING SCORECARD

List three ideas from this chapter that you will put into immediate use to begin obtaining the results you seek.

☐ *Idea:*

_____

_____

_____

Start Date: _____

Finish Line Date: _____

☐ *Idea:*

_____

_____

_____

Start Date: _____

Finish Line Date: _____

☐ *Idea:*

_____

_____

_____

Start Date: _____

Finish Line Date: _____

EVENT:

RAPPORT

chapter 5

P-R-<u>A</u>-C-T-I-C-E
Attention

You are ready to begin a conversation with a prospective buyer. Now it is crunch time! You have to work hard to ensure a buyer will want to talk to you. You must make a solid first impression since you will not get the opportunity for a second first impression. So what do you do?

To get attention you must command attention. This begins with some physical as well as mental attributes. The following are only suggestions, but I encourage you to carefully consider them. Sometimes the subtleties are all you need to set you apart from your competition.

■ Phone Voice

In the previous chapter I spoke about gaining rapport. Rapport is the implicit connection parties provide to communicate with each other. Voice is very much a part of building rapport. Your phone voice must be pleasant and professional. The information you present must be well planned and perhaps scripted. Understand I am not suggesting that you read from a script but, similar to calling the account, you must have an idea of the items you want to present to the prospect.

■ Dress Code

Dress codes in 2006 (publishing date of this book) are different today then they were 10 years ago. Many corporations had a standard dress such as suit and tie for gentlemen and suit or blouse and skirt for ladies. Today, the landscape is different. Business casual has taken command.

Business casual is a style of dress requiring trousers and button down or polo shirt for men and pants and a nice blouse or polo shirt for women. There are some nuances to this. Many organizations are lackadaisical in administering their required dress code. Rather then spend time on the fashion trends, I will use this chapter to make recommendations.

Shoes—always have a nicely shined pair of shoes. Many people size up individuals from the floor to the head. If the floor is first, then you better make the first impression the best. Shoes must also match the attire that you are wearing. While I subscribe to being fashionable, something wild and ostentatious will cast more shadows then compliments. Remember, "Better to be safe then sorry."

Seams—trousers and slacks should be neatly pressed. Nice seams in the middle of the quadriceps look very nice and fashionable. Gentlemen should avoid loose change in the pocket, keys and a large wallet.

Shirts—shirts and blouses should also be pressed. Both should match the trousers. Avoid wild colors, and shirts that "advertise." A company shirt with a logo is fine, but avoid too many. Similar to trousers avoid placing pens, pencils, notes, etc. in front pockets.

Client's Dress Code—most important, if you are visiting with a client the first time, always ask them about the dress code. Ask about their culture and how business is conducted. This will give you a sense of attitude, team play, communication and morale. By asking, you will immediately fit in to the company culture by blending. By the way, blending is also a form of building rapport and it is important to getting attention. You want to make that favorable first impression so a prospective buyer is saying "Now this is a smart sales professional. They dress sharp, they look professional, and they are worth listening to."

Jewelry—be cautious with the amount of jewelry you wear. Certainly jewelry is appropriate and meant to be worn. But be careful about being too flashy. This includes watches, rings, necklaces, etc. I recommend conservatism and caution. The cliché goes, "Less is more."

Now that I have addressed some of the personal aspects of gaining attention let me take you through some of the professional aspects so that you not only gain clients' attention, you hold it so you can move clients through the PRACTICE™ process.

One of the first methods of getting attention is to continue to build rapport, and one of the most successful methods, as we discussed in the previous chapter, is to ask questions. Get to know your prospective buyer and get to understand their reasons for meeting you. Engage your prospect's attention by discussing something that interests them.

Many sales professionals open with the same cliché, "Hi I am so and so and I am here…" The buyer does not want the biographical data. The buyer wants useful information and how it will assist them now! A better opening statement might be, "I have noticed that attrition is very high in your industry, what systems are in place to reverse this trend?" This is a statement that is business oriented and focuses the attention on the issues and attitudes within the buyer account. Remember, "What's in it for me," dominates when selling.

■ Question Bearing on a Need

From a course I had taken many years ago with Dale Carnegie and Associates, the statement of *question bearing on a need* brings particular interest from buyers. When you ask a question that relates to their needs and focuses on their pains it begins to tilt the conversation from a judgmental perspective to one of "Hey, this person might be able to assist me and my issue."

The question bearing on a need creates immediate action from the buyer and engages them. If the buyer engages with you, you have their attention and you can quickly begin interacting to resolve issues. Additionally, this question opener is very easy; the most difficult part might be to frame the question. However, once asked, all you need to do is sit back and listen to the customer.

■ Statistical/Factual Information

While questioning is a good way to begin, so is *information presentation*. With information you need to be cautious since your buyer might not be ready to receive this material. Or, their personality profile (as discussed in the Rapport Chapter) is one that does not need statistical information. However, there are times when factual information can prove to be quite useful.

To exemplify, "Mr. Buyer are you aware that in a recent study on Salary.com 65% of employees expect to seek a new job in the next three months?" This is very useful information and very helpful to you. It illustrates that you have done your homework. It helps you immediately focus on the pain of the client. Facts enable you to engage the client if they enjoy these statistics. Additionally, facts and figures can be very surprising and can validate you and your company.

Numerical information and facts are quite striking if delivered well. They will certainly gain attention from your buyer. Be a bit cautious. Ensure with the stated example, or your own, that you have additional information such as when the study was completed and how many participated.

You might want to have the study with you to assist in supplying this useful information to buyers. In fact, from time to time I recommend that you give your buyer copies of industry or news articles. They might not have seen the content and it will solidify your experience with the industry, the company, and the buyer needs. Remember, anything you can do to separate yourself from the competition will be better for you.

■ *Curiosity*

To begin the conversation you need to suggest to the buyer something that arouses curiosity and appeal. If relevant, statistics can be an effective attention getter.

If you are selling computers you might ask the client if they heard of the latest innovation that will rock the industry. Or you might arouse curiosity by referring to a new computer memory chip that is much faster. Most likely, the buyer will be intrigued and will continue to ask questions about where the information developed and when the product might be on the market.

■ Referral

In other chapters you will read about my moniker for closing sales. What always separates a good sales professional from a great sales professional is my other moniker: *AGR*, pronounced ARG! Always get referrals. Referral selling is so important today. With innovations in technology and the need to give time and attention to new clients, sales professionals require the slightest edge to remain effective.

If done correctly and with integrity, referral selling can be a mainstay for your business. You might not need to cold call, research, and collect data if your present clients are leading the way for you. However, you must be careful not to overuse your referrals. Also, you must not be surreptitious and name drop whenever you believe you can. Be cautious and walk a fine line, but do use referrals—they are your best calling card.

Referrals can be direct or indirect. Directly, you are provided with a name from one of your existing clients or peers. You contact your client using that person's name. Indirectly, (and this works well too), you might mention that you are working with clients located in a similar area or, more importantly, in a similar industry. This technique is helpful as competitors always want to know what the other is doing to get the "edge." These methods always gain attention!

■ Newsworthy

Similar to statistical information and facts, newsworthy content always attracts clients' attention. Sales professionals have to be like squirrels in winter, always stacking the nuts in case you need them. Gather any and all relevant information and pass it on when needed. Read books, trade publications, newspapers, or subscribe to an electronic clipping service or the new term is *RSS* (Really Simple Syndication), a format designed for sharing headlines and other Web content) feed. You might also gain information from a trade association, competitors or even other sales professionals.

Everyone wants to be in the know and the sooner you can get information into their hands the better. If it is interesting the buyer will want to hear it. However, I encourage you to be cautious: pass around information, *not* rumor or speculation. There is plenty of the latter in the world, but buyers can never have enough good substantial information.

■ *Value*

Everyone will be open to those that are helpful and willing to assist. A selling professional who comes with suggestions provides value. You might use a combination of ideas mentioned in this chapter or you might have your own. No matter which way you choose, do something, say something and be someone that provides clear value to the buyer. In fact that is what buyers seek—clarity; help them find it.

Uncover opportunities for clients and don't be ashamed to tell them. If the client values you and your service, they will value the ideas that you bring to them. Use many of the ideas mentioned in the preparation chapter. Seek opportunities in news, trade journals, the gym, anywhere you can to glean information useful for your buyer.

If you do not get attention, you will never get to the other phases of PRACTICE™. If you cannot get attention from a buyer, you get nothing. Many people shy away from this step thinking that it is not a big deal to get in front of a prospect. In today's time-sensitive and competitive world it most certainly is a big deal. It is vital that you get their attention and quickly!

Further, no two clients are the same so you will need to be familiar with a variety of techniques to engage the other party. You want the person to think you are a professional, you are sharp, you have presence and personality, and, more importantly, you are worth listening to!

Now we move from Attention to Convincing them that you are not only worth listening to, but understand the answer to their pain. Moreover, your services can diminish their pain!

> *"Don't pay any attention to what they write about you.*
> *Just measure it in inches."*
> —Andy Warhol

People ➤ Problem ➤ Personal

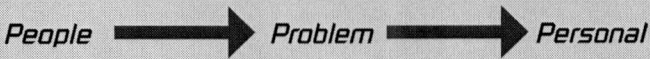

O – Original Idea

P – Personal Question

E - Educational

N – Negative Statement

E – Enthusiasm for the Client

R - Referral

Questions to ask the prospect:

Personal Questions:

1. _____

2. _____

3. _____

4. _____

Problem Questions:

1. _____

2. _____

3. _____

4. _____

Question Bearing on a Need:

1. _____

2. _____

3. _____

4. _____

SELLING SCORECARD

List three ideas from this chapter that you will put into immediate use to begin obtaining the results you seek.

☐ **Idea:**

_____

_____

_____

Start Date: _____

Finish Line Date: _____

☐ **Idea:**

_____

_____

_____

Start Date: _____

Finish Line Date: _____

☐ **Idea:**

_____

_____

_____

Start Date: _____

Finish Line Date: _____

EVENT:

ATTENTION

chapter 6

P-R-A-<u>C</u>-T-I-C-E
Convincing

O nce you have developed rapport with the client, the next step is to convince him or her that your product or service is worthy. One of the basic techniques involves presenting the product's benefits.

As you work to convince your client of the need to purchase from you, be careful to provide only the facts that are germane to the sale. Remember, less is more, and too many options may confuse and frustrate the buyer.

Equally important is the ability to support your claims with testimonials, statistics, or other information that assists the client in determining that your product is genuinely appropriate for his or her needs. When convincing a buyer speak factually and passionately. You must truly believe in your product or service.

A passionate and factual salesperson can make an emotional appeal, implying that the buyer is making the right decision: "This is the product for you!" Clients can read your body language and they can hear conviction in your voice. If you believe in the credibility of your product, the buyer will, too.

■ Ask Questions

During this process, it is important to ask questions, and lots of them! As you read this book, you will find numerous instances where I discuss the importance of asking appropriate questions. Why? Because good questioning skills are crucial for sales success. And yet, your ability to be quiet and listen for the reply is equally important. Based on what you hear, guide the conversation to lay the groundwork for the methods you will use to convince the client to buy.

I recall being told of a meeting between a sales professional and a client. The buyer sat back, listening to the presentation. After several moments, the buyer became very interested in the product. As his interest grew, he began to ask questions. However, any time he posed a question, the sales professional interjected more about the product. The buyer never received the answers he sought and the sale was lost. The moral of the story is clear: When a client speaks, close your mouth and listen!

■ *Demonstrate Solutions*

Convince is synonymous with demonstrate, which is defined as: "to illustrate and explain, especially with many examples." During this step of the sales process, you may employ many items to get your point across. These props may help show the client specific product features and benefits.

While features and benefits are discussed in more detail later, a quick explanation will assist you. A feature is something that a product can do. A benefit answers the clients' question, "What's in it for me?"

Buyers do not purchase features. Instead, they purchase solutions to their problems. They purchase benefits. Therefore, when you are convincing the client to buy, it is imperative to demonstrate how the product's features provide the benefits the client seeks.

This is where good listening omes in. Each presentation must be geared to the individual buyer. Thus, you must listen carefully to make sure you address the buyer's concerns and desires through the solutions available via your product or service.

As you present information, use concise sentences, such as, "Seventy-four percent of entrepreneurs interviewed use this printer." This sentence contains a form of evidence. It is based on the need of the client to know who else uses the printer, and it implicitly illustrates that if the buyer makes the purchase he or she will be in good company.

To make sure the client understands the information your present, remember to use the *C3 Formula*: be clear, concise, and consistent.

The first of the three C's, clarity, speaks for itself. No one will make a purchase based on muddled and confusing information.

Second, consider the axiom used in geometry: "The shortest distance between any two points is a straight line." This is also true in selling. Be concise by making your points in short bursts punctuated by pauses so that the buyer can absorb the information.

Finally, your delivery must be consistent. Picture yourself as the conductor of an orchestra, and be very rhythmic in your approach: Deliver, pause, deliver, pause, etc. Maintain a consistent level of volume and pitch as you speak, but don't use an expressionless monotone.

■ Golden Moments—Features and Benefits

One of the most common problems of sales professionals is the inability to separate features from benefits. As I've already emphasized, buyers purchase products based on perceived benefits, not simply on a conglomeration of meaningless features.

Presenting features without tying them to associated benefits is like trying to sell ice cream without a cup or cone. Sales professionals must relate features to the benefits they provide. Doing so is the only way to make and close the sale.

Norman Strauss was one of the best sales trainers I knew. He excelled at asking pertinent questions. "Keep asking the client if he wants to know what the product will do for him," Norman advised. However, benefits alone do little; to give them credibility, you must link benefits with the features that produce them.

You can present features by describing specific aspects of a product or service. Follow this with a transitional phrase, also known as a bridge, that links the feature to its benefit. For instance:

■ What this means to you…

■ The benefit to you is…

■ The reason why I mention this is…

■ This provides you with…

■ So that…

These statements will help you link the feature to the corresponding benefit. An other reason for linking features and benefits is that you can connect a benefit directly to the buyer, not just to the general public. It is your professional mission to demonstrate how your product's benefits will serve the buyer's needs.

Many sales professionals do not adequately connect their products' features and benefits. It is easy to simply mention that the car comes in blue, or the computer runs quickly. But this is usually not enough to make a sale.

You may be familiar with the 80/20 Rule, also known as the Paretto Principle. Using this principle, we can assume that 80 percent of sales professionals do not use a benefit statement. Of that 80 percent, only 20 percent will close the sale. Meanwhile, of the 20 percent who do use benefit statements, 80 percent will close the sale.

The chart below will help you identify features and their associated benefits. Simply list all the features of your product or service, identify a bridge from the examples above or of your own creation, and then list the corresponding benefits. Features and benefits are vital, and the more you can identify, the more flexible you can be in tailoring your presentations and negotiations to meet the client's needs.

Feature	Bridges	Benefit

■ Feature Bridges Benefit

People need evidence in order to make a fully informed decision. The best sales professionals present multiple forms of evidence to support their statements regarding a product's potential benefits to the buyer.

Each sales call is different and you'll require various types of evidence in each situation. To assist you in remembering the wide array of evidence types available for your use, keep this acronym in mind: *EAGER TREATS*:

E	Example	Typical way in which the product is used.
A	Analogy	Describe how one might use the product.
G	Graphs	To visually describe usage and statistics.
E	Exhibits	Illustration of the product in use.
R	Referral	Nothing is better than a satisfied client.
T	Testimonial	Good clients are your best sales tools.
R	Real Stories	Depict the service in use—use someone in a situation similar to that of the client.
E	Evidence	Truthful details about a product in use.
A	Annual Report	Helps position the company and its personnel.
T	True Statement	Case studies are very useful.
S	Statistics	Analytical people seek additional knowledge.

Using various types of evidence to convince buyers of their need for your product is similar to having a solid base of features and benefits. You need enough variety so that you can tailor your sales presentation for each buyer and sales situation. More importantly, you should become an evidence collector and amass as many forms of evidence as possible to support your product's claims. One can never have too many tools in the tool bag.

Use the chart on the next page to write examples of each type of evidence as it relates to your product or service. You can then draw upon these notes as you prepare for upcoming sales presentations.

Example: _____

Analogy: _____

Graphs: _____

Exhibits: _____

Referral: _____

Testimonial: _____

Real Stories: _____

Evidence: _____

Annual Report: _____

True Statement: _____

Statistics: _____

These strategies are most helpful when you are trying to close the sale with an indecisive buyer. For example, if the buyer is resisting your attempts to close the sale, toss him or her some EAGER TREATS. Perhaps you have not yet honed in on the correct form of evidence that will sway the client.

If a client appears to be wavering in the purchase decision, don't forget to ask, "Is this the type of service that you seek?" It is a good idea to ask for your client's thoughts frequently and to affirm their interest. As Dale Carnegie taught, your ability to continually get the "yes" will move you closer and closer to the sale.

> *"We can have facts without thinking,
> but we cannot have thinking without facts."*
>
> —John Dewey (1859-1952)

Evidence	Feature	Bridge	Benefit

E	Example	
A	Analogy	
G	Graphs	
E	Exhibits	
R	Referral	
T	Testimonial	
R	Real Stories	
E	Evidence	
A	Annual Report	
T	True Statement	
S	Statistics	

SELLING SCORECARD

List three ideas from this chapter that you will put into immediate use to begin obtaining the results you seek.

☐ **Idea:**

_____

_____

_____

Start Date: _____

Finish Line Date: _____

EVENT:

☐ **Idea:**

_____

_____

_____

Start Date: _____

Finish Line Date: _____

☐ **Idea:**

_____

_____

_____

Start Date: _____

Finish Line Date: _____

CONVINCING

chapter 7

P-R-A-C-T-I-C-E
Time
Management

Have you every wondered why you are not making enough money? Have you ever gotten to work and wonder why the sales professional next to you is admired? Do you believe it is fate, dumb luck, or fortune?

Are you tired of being second person on the sales team? Do you want to know what the differences are between top sales representatives and you? Are you interested in becoming number one?

If so, I can tell you that in my many years of sales consulting and training I have seen good and I have seen great sales professionals. For me, the differences in the two types of individuals come down to the efficiency in time management. Proper sales time management not only saves time by avoiding wasteful client calls but it enables you to make more money! After all, that is what you want, isn't it?

Simply put—successful and motivated sales professionals do not procrastinate. They use time as the tool to keep them focused and honor their commitments to meet revenue and customer expectations. Success comes from not wasting time and from blocking in areas of the day to accomplish tasks aligned with the business mission and revenue goals.

You will not see successful people cajoling at the water cooler, chatting on the telephone with friends nor wasting time with many administrative tasks. These folks plan their work and work their plan. I am not saying that they do not have fun. They simply know that there's a time to work and a time to play.

Essentially, sales professionals in this category are the CEO's of their destiny. They operate their desk as an independent business, focused on profit and horrified at loss.

■ *Spend Your 86,400 Wisely*

Sales people are extremely goal oriented and good time managers. Goals are the drivers of effective sales professionals. They assist in providing a road map for guidance as well as success.

Harvey McKay, the author of *Swim with the Sharks*, once stated that goals are nothing more than dreams with a time frame. Yet for successful sales professionals their dreams become reality.

Sales people know how many people to call, how many appointments to make, and how many items they need to sell in order to exceed, not just make quota. Believe it or not, money is not the success factor of a great sales professional, it is the achievement of goals.

Sales professionals, because of their goal orientation, operate in blocks of time. In fact, good sales people spend 65% of their time in front of customers and the remainder of their time on travel, business reports, phone follow-up and writing orders. Further, sales professionals are not driven by a clock, they keep going to accomplish their mission and stay they plan until they meet their objectives. They believe that sales is a 24-hour process.

What would you do if given $86,400, which you had to spend during the next 24 hours? Would you buy a new automobile? How about that motorcycle you are longing for? What about dinner at a five-star restaurant? Would you like a new dress or a new suit? How about just going on an all-day spending spree? I'm sure you could find plenty of ways to use the money.

Many people say they would invest the money, put it away for retirement, pay off debts, or put it into a savings account.

Are you aware that in a given day, we have 86,400 seconds provided by the bank of life? We must use the time wisely because at the close of the day, it is gone forever. So I now ask, when you are given 24 hours to spend 86,400 seconds, how do you spend your day?

The difference between our attitudes regarding money and time is interesting: we want to invest money and spend time. Yet if time is so important, then why do we spend it carelessly? Perhaps we need to take a closer look at spending time wisely so we can create more success in our lives.

■ *The SMART Way to Achieve Goals*

It is time to take hold of your priorities and make them actionable. You must have a plan to move forward in getting your priorities in order. That plan begins with goals.

As mentioned on page 31, goals will help you answer three vital questions:

- ■ Who are you?

- ■ Where are you going?

- ■ How will you get there?

Think for a moment about the age-old story of Ebenezer Scrooge, from Charles Dickens' *A Christmas Carol.* Scrooge is an old codger who does not like anyone, perhaps even himself. He is nasty to everyone: friends, family, neighbors, and even strangers. He does not engage in conversation, nor is he nice when he is engaged. If you do not appreciate where you are in life, it's very possible to be like Scrooge, and simply crawl into your hole and avoid all who try to befriend you.

Scrooge went to bed early on Christmas Eve and had a very disturbing night. He envisioned himself being visited by the ghosts of Christmas Past, Present, and Future. When each ghost took Scrooge to a different period from his life, he was dismayed by what he saw. The experience forced him to take note of his unhappiness, anger, depression, and overall lack of control.

Does your life resemble that of Ebenezer Scrooge? If I took a picture of your life before you read this book, would you like what you saw, or would you want to make some changes? Scrooge changed his life, and so can you!

The first step in setting goals and remaking your future is to learn how to be *SMART.*

SMART is an acronym that you can use to make your goals achievable. SMART goals allow you to maintain focus and pace, while expediting results for rapid success.

SMART stands for: Specific, Measurable, Achievable, Realistic, and Time Frame.

To begin creating a SMART goal, identify something you want to accomplish in no more than 12 weeks. For example, let's say that you want to call upon the CFO of a multinational organization. The purpose of your call is to present your product and its benefits. And you want to do this at some point during the next six weeks. By using the SMART formula, you achieve your goal.

■ **S**—Specific

Current Version: I want to meet a CFO.

SMART Version: I will meet Vernon Smith, CFO of Getting to the Finish Line, so that I can begin to establish a business relationship with his firm.

■ **M**—Measurable

Current Version: I will call every day.

SMART Version: I will research the company so that I can identify some of Mr. Smith's needs. My research will help me establish immediate rapport on the telephone.

■ **A**—Achievable

Current Version: Guess so.

SMART Version: As long as I establish a mission, a vision, a motive, and benefits, I can achieve this meeting.

- **R**—Realistic

Current Version: Sure, why not?

SMART Version: As long as I stick to my plan, set a time frame, and do not procrastinate, I can achieve this goal.

- **T**—Time Frame

Current Version: As soon as possible.

SMART Version: I will make this call on June 14 at 3:30 p.m.

Below is an example of a SMART MAP to help plan your day.

Goals

- **S**: _____
- **M**: _____
- **A**: _____
- **R**: _____
- **T**: _____

Teammates:	*Spectators*:
Identify things/people to help your reach your goals:	Identify things/people that hold you back from reaching your goals:
_____	_____
_____	_____
_____	_____
_____	_____
_____	_____
_____	_____

A few final thoughts about goals: first, you must never criticize yourself if you do not reach a goal by your target date. Goals sometimes need adjusting in relation to circumstances. It's not advisable to rush crucial steps toward your goal in order to meet a self-imposed time frame.

Second, there will be many who want to prevent you from reaching your goal. Why? Perhaps for a reason as basic as envy. You must remain focused if you want to accomplish what you set out to do, and you must remain determined to achieve your success, despite the naysayers.

Sales professionals set goals for accounts they want to penetrate, people they want to talk with, and money they want to make. Sales goals are nothing more than personal dreams. They are yours and yours alone. Avoid those that believe you will not reach your destiny.

■ *Teammates & Specators*

There is one important thing you can do to help avoid these distractions: identify them. When you write your goals using the SMART formula, you must identify the issues that could hinder your success and those that could help you reach success. I call these factors *Teammates* and *Spectators*.

Teammates are people or circumstances that aid you in reaching your goal. Examples are time management, research, weather, health, mental toughness, and breaking things down into smaller tasks. To help you on the road to success, list seven to ten potential teammates.

Spectators are people or circumstances that distract you, discourage you, and disorient you, preventing you from reaching your goal. Examples include weather, health, friends, food, drugs, alcohol, and procrastination. To help you on the road to success, list seven to ten potential spectators.

■ *Visualize Results*

Earlier in the text I wrote about visualization as an effective tool you can use to prepare yourself for sales success. This also works well as an adjunct to your SMART goal-setting.

Sit in a quiet room and close your eyes. When you are completely quiet, relaxed, and focused on your mission, envision your success. What does it look like? What are you wearing? How do you feel? Who is near you? Feel yourself with the goal completed. Feel and sense the elation: let your nervous system and your insides explode with the accomplishment!

Finally, when you reach your goal, reward yourself. You work hard to achieve your aspirations; give yourself credit! The next time you open a new account, call a prospective client, or finalize an important proposal, give yourself the gift of a pat on the back—you deserve it!

Getting to the Finish Line is about results, and when you can see the results of your hard work, whether it is professional or personal, you will accomplish more than you ever thought possible.

■ Procrastination

Our focus on time management cannot be considered complete without a discussion of procrastination, putting off dealing with something stressful or important. Perhaps the biggest factor that throws us off track in reaching our goals is procrastination.

Procrastination is fundamentally about fear. You can add *FEAR* to your list of handy acronyms: *False Experiences Appearing Real.* When you procrastinate, you are fearful of both success and failure.

For some, the fear of success can be bewildering, and you might be uncertain what will happen if you do succeed. You cannot imagine the future and are fearful of what it holds. Fear of success is something that must be overcome or you will never achieve anything.

On the other hand, fear to the person fixated on failure is a phobia of stumbling, lack of acceptance, delay, and inability to meet expectations. Fear deters us from creation, growth, and gain. When we overcome fear, we can overcome more than we ever thought possible and develop growth opportunities for present and future success.

■ Overcoming Fear Through Visualization

As I described earlier, I first discovered visualization during my days running track and field. For me, visualization helped take my goals and aspirations to the next level and advanced my athletic career. I remain a staunch believer in the power of visualization.

Visualization is often used as a psychological tool for those who are overcoming phobias or bad habits. Although I mentioned basic visualization techniques in previous chapters, I want to review this process again in slightly more detail:

Sitting or laying down, begin to breathe deeply and slowly. Feel your breath enter your abdomen. Your belly should rise as you inhale and fall as you exhale. This is known as diaphragmatic breathing, and it oxygenates the body while helping to relax tense muscles. You may want to play soft music in the background – nature sounds and quiet chords may help you relax.

Let your body relax, concentrating on how your body feels, how loose your muscles and tendons have become. Feel the weight of your extremities, feel your pulse, and remain aware of your breathing. You might even want to recite a relaxing mantra or chant, such as, "Breathe, relax, now be free; Breathe, relax, now be free."

Once you are in a state of total concentration and relaxation, begin to visualize yourself achieving one of your goals or overcoming a fearful situation. See yourself and notice the clothes you are wearing, the smell of your cologne, and the warmth of the air around you. Begin to view the environment where you are located. What does the air smell like? Are there people with you? What pictures are hanging on the wall? What cars do you see? What food or drinks are available? Is it a cloudy or sunny day?

Have you ever had a deja vu moment? Have you ever mysteriously and intuitively felt convinced that you had been someplace before? That is what visualization is like. You can create your own future through this powerful practice.

Ten to fifteen minutes a few times per week is all that's needed to incorporate this life-changing tool into your daily routine.

▪ *Prioritization*

"The effective person does the important things first. And has less urgent battles and crises that arise!"

One of the most important steps for anyone, especially sales profession-als, is prioritization. The cliché time is money, reigns as the guidepost for most selling professionals. Time is the one item you do not get to reinvent, nor get back. Once it is gone, that is it. Therefore, sales profes-sionals must use their time sparingly and efficiently.

The reward for managing your time is the enrichment of not only your professional life, but your personal life. And, good time management also gets you closer to your selling goals. Sales people must focus on their highest priorities and consistently place them first. The added ben-efit of a well-organized work schedule is the creation of time for family, friends, and the leisure activities that rejuvenate and refresh you.

With only 24 hours in a day, how can all the calls, the reports and the sales get completed? Simply put, planning. Planning is a vital aspect of every professional salesperson's career. It is there that efficiency is born. Sales professionals should plan the order of their calls so as not to retrace steps; they should plan when to respond to email. They might even plan where and when to visit with certain clients to reduce time in airports or behind the window of an automobile.

Typically, most of us respond to what we believe are urgent matters and forget to pre-plan and be proactive. By reacting to issues sales people become Emergency Medical Technicians for all incoming work. The red light goes on and sales people scurry to get THAT item completed im-mediately.

Proactive planning and working on important, yet not urgent, informa-tion makes the day less daunting and enables a sales professional to get more accomplished in less time. Consider that there are only 24 hours in a day. If the sales person responds to all that comes to them; they will never accomplish any of their important items and they will never have balance at work or at home. Why? They will not be at home because of all the work in the office.

This chart illustrates that with only 24 hours per day to accomplish things, sales professionals must be more aware of where their time is spent. Notice that many times we work from four areas, urgent, important, not urgent and not important.

Setting Priorities

Sales professionals especially tend to work from the idea that all things are urgent and react to all things that come to them. There are also times when sales professionals procrastinate and do not take care of the important items. They spend time working on tasks that are not important. The only way to get more done in less time is to prioritize and work on those things that are important first. This will take you from reactive mode to proactive and enable you to get more accomplished in less time.

One of the first items for a sales person is to plan calls either in the morning or in the afternoon. Sporadically making appointments during the day leaves less room for other important things.

Second, sales professionals should only reply to telephone calls and emails four to five times per day, and these should be grouped. Too many sales people respond to all calls coming to them and that too leaves less room to respond to other items on the daily agenda.

Third prioritize your tasks using numbers and color coding. Red for urgent, Yellow for important but not urgent, and Green for personal or not important or urgent. You can place your list on a piece of paper or simply obtain colored manila folders to organize your work. Then when you finally group the list in order of importance, organize the list in numerical order. Place a number on the top of the paper of the task and number in chronological order the importance in which you need to complete the task. The trick is to have no more than three items in each color group or a total of nine items in one day; mainly because you will not have the time to complete them.

One final item to help you with prioritization is something that constantly stares you in the face, the items you hate to do. You put it off and put it off but never get it off your To Do List. However there is a way out!

■ Things to Do/Things to Avoid

One of the greatest ideas I ever heard came from motivational speaker Nido Quebin. He said in order to save yourself the headache of to-do lists, make a not-to-do list.

This simple technique can save you time, hassle, and headaches. Write down all of the things that waste your time in a given sales day. These can range from reading the daily paper to watching the news; from chatting with colleagues, clients, and peers to reading unnecessary emails.

Once you have your list complete, place it in a spot where you will see it every day: on a bathroom mirror, next to a telephone, or personal computer, for example. The more you see the list, the more often you will be reminded of the things that waste your time so that you can avoid those things and allocate your resources wisely.

■ Time Management

Goals, lists, and visualization are all techniques to help you get control of your time. And they are tools that aid in your organizational success. There is one final item to assist your sales day: good foundational time management.

We started this section with the bank of life and the idea that you only have 86,400 seconds to spend in your day. You then must allocate these items by priority so that you can move your life toward a more rewarding balance.

Time management begins with these simple truths: things are urgent or not urgent; important or not important. Each day your professional and personal life revolves around these four areas where people control you and you strive to control others. Things may always be in crisis mode, or you may be perpetually overcome by interruptions. You also will often experience a procrastinator amongst your crowd.

So if you are seeking ways to overcome the crises or the interruptions, simply begin to prioritize your day. Prioritize everything and make appointments. This includes lunch.

How do you do this? Label your entire day's schedule with codes. Everything in your day, appointments, email, phone calls, lunch, children to soccer practice, and writing proposals all get coded, both alphabetically and then numerically.

To begin, all items get coded with an alphabetic letter.

- **A**—Red Hot. The item requires completion within a 12- to 24-hour time frame.

- **B**—Very Important. The task requires completion within a 24- to 48-hour timeframe.

- **C**—Important. The task requires completion within 48 to 72 hours or by the end of the week.

Once you have coded your daily items in this way, use numbers to further assess their importance.

You will never have more than three items in each category. And your categories will never go past the letter C. You need to restrict yourself to no more than nine items per day. You cannot handle more than this, and trying to do too much only prevents you from getting important things completed.

Further, by trying to accomplish more than this, you only end up rolling items from one day to the next, thereby piling on more things. That's how you got where you are now: confused and stressed because you're not getting important, high-priority tasks accomplished on time.

You do not have to purchase a software program or a new book to apply this technique. Simply begin to list all of the items you need to do each day and code them appropriately. Once you begin to see the usefulness of this exercise and experience the related stress reduction, your habits will change, and you will notice more free time in your life.

Finally, when you prioritize you should also take into consideration those things you do not like to do such as phone calls, sales reports, call sheets, and answering emails. Do the things you hate to do first. Once those tasks are completed, the entire day will go uphill. Why? Simply because you have taken away that which you deplore, leaving the remainder of the day filled with enjoyable tasks.

■ Sales Call Planning

Planning is one of the keys to your success. One rule of thumb to keep in mind is that Finish Line selling is about strategy and planning, not speed. You must think through each and every situation so that you are always aware of issues around you. As a sales professional, you are surrounded by the forces of competition: the marketplace, the companies you seek to service, your employer, and even your own personal issues. It is imperative that you remain aware of these issues and take appropriate steps to plan for each and every portion of your success.

The Sales Planning Guide, on pages 38 to 40, is an extremely valuable tool for analyzing customers. It enables you to understand the tips and techniques that can get you to the finish line and to harness external forces affecting the sales situation in a way that advances your progress.

To use the Planning Guide, begin by identifying the customer and the role of your contact within the company. You can then formulate strategic plans so that when you come upon a hurdle, you can jump it without much difficulty.

List the pertinent information regarding your client. This includes the company name, type of industry, and contact identification. When you have completed this section, take a few moments to think about your client's business needs and how you can help to fulfill those needs. What can you bring to the table when you meet with your client? This step is vital. I have seen many sales professionals fail to even reach the starting line because they do not adequately plan or have a clear agenda for their sales calls. In addition, you must understand the issues on both sides before you meet face-to-face. Selling is multidimensional; you must know your role and the role of your client. This guide makes you take on two roles: your own, and those of your clients. Emulate the client. Wear his or her figurative shoes and understand the issues he or she faces so you can be of better service.

Next, list all other individuals involved in the decision-making process so you recognize those who can coach you as well as those who can impede your Finish Line success. Some of the people you will meet with have different roles and responsibilities in the process. As I have previously described, these roles include the gatekeeper, the decision-maker, the recommender, the influencer, the coach, and the check writer.

Finally, list the features and benefits of your product or service, the dominant buying motive your client should have for purchase, and the possible objections that he or she might raise. Your preparation before each and every call will save you time, energy, and most of all headaches down the road.

■ *Time to Change Habits*

As you can see from this chapter, sound time management is not about tricks but solid techniques that give you more time and less stress. However, be aware that the transition to these techniques requires the changing of many personal habits that you employed most of your life. You will need to learn how to change these habits.

To implement change, you need to develop routines three to four times per day, three times per week during a 30-day period. It has been said that what gets repeated gets rewarded, and this is true. Repetition will aid in change. Repetition will spark development. Repetition will create new ways of doing things. Follow the strategies listed above, and you are guaranteed to arrive at the Finish Line!

> *"An organization that is strong and stable and is ready to commit time, money, and patience will be more apt to reap rewards than the quick-hitting opportunist."*
>
> —Richard Miller, *The Direct Marketing Handbook*

SELF-QUIZ: EXAMINING YOUR GOAL ORIENTATION

After reading each of the following statements, circle the number that corresponds to whether you agree (3), are not certain (2) or disagree (1):

1. I have a personal mission statement	3	2	1
2. I have written goals and objectives	3	2	1
3. I have set goals and objectives	3	2	1
4. I have written goals for my career	3	2	1
5. I keep track of my interruptions during the day	3	2	1
6. I sometimes get lost in my quest	3	2	1
7. I do not have any mentors	3	2	1
8. I do not have enough time in a day to get everything done	3	2	1
9. I get down on myself for not knowing my quest.	3	2	1
10. I know what I want my epitaph to say.	3	2	1

Add up your scores to help define where you are in the goal management grid. This will help you understand where you are and where you need to begin.

22 or more = You know where you are going

21 to 14 = With a bit of planning you are on the right page

Less than 14 = You need to establish goals and objectives to set a path in your life

The 80/20 Rule

20% of the effort will obtain 80% of the results

80% of the results come from 20% of the effort

The majority of your time at work should be spent on activities like:

P—Preparation

P—Prevention

P—Planning

R—Relationship-building

ACTIVITY: Create a list of your daily routines (include *everything* you do).

☐ _____

☐ _____

☐ _____

☐ _____

☐ _____

☐ _____

☐ _____

☐ _____

☐ _____

☐ _____

☐ _____

☐ _____

☐ _____

☐ _____

☐ _____

☐ _____

☐ _____

☐ _____

☐ _____

Check the activities that fall in the 20% category.

TIME MANAGEMENT

Take along, hard look at the rest of your activities. Where are you wasting time? What steps will you take to use your time more effectively? List those below.

Time wasting activities:

_____

_____

_____

_____

Steps to take to use time effectively:

_____

_____

_____

_____

What one thing could you do (aren't doing now) that if you did on regular basis, would make a tremendous positive difference in your personal life?

_____

_____

What one thing in your business or professional life would bring similar results?

_____

_____

TIME MANAGEMENT

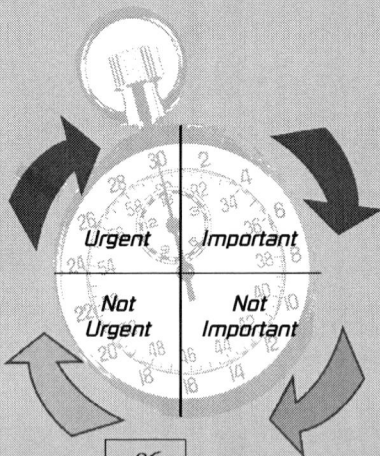

What are some of your priorities that are in your **Urgent** quadrant right now?

_____

_____

_____

What are some of your priorities that are in your **Important** quadrant now?

_____

_____

_____

What are some of your priorities that are in your **Not Important** quadrant now?

_____

_____

Which of these priorities can you eliminate?

_____

_____

What are some of your priorities that are in your **Not Urgent** quadrant now?

_____

_____

What steps will you take to get rid of these priorities?

_____

_____

In which quadrant are you investing the majority of your time?

_____

_____

Is this the most effective use of your time? Why or why not?

_____

_____

TIME MANAGEMENT

87

Habit Identifier

MY BAD HABITS   **IDEAS THAT INSPIRE RESULTS**

_____   _____

_____   _____

_____   _____

_____   _____

_____   _____

_____   _____

_____   _____

_____   _____

_____   _____

_____   _____

_____   _____

_____   _____

_____   _____

Keep in mind that it takes 21 days to make or change a habit.

1	2	3	4	5
6	7	8	9	10
11	12	13	14	15
16	17	18	19	20
21				

SELLING SCORECARD

List three ideas from this chapter that you will put into immediate use to begin obtaining the results you seek.

☐ **Idea:**

_____

_____

_____

Start Date: _____

Finish Line Date: _____

☐ **Idea:**

_____

_____

_____

Start Date: _____

Finish Line Date: _____

☐ **Idea:**

_____

_____

_____

Start Date: _____

Finish Line Date: _____

EVENT:

TIME MANAGEMENT

chapter 8

P-R-A-C-T-I-C-E
Interest

Pursuit and attainment of interest is perhaps one of the easiest steps in the selling process. Why? Because, as we touched upon when covering features and benefits, you simply need to talk about what the product or service will do for the client.

In today's time-sensitive world, it might be hard to concentrate solely on the prospect. However, for just a few moments, turn your mind from yourself to the client. I always tell my clients that the secret to sales and marketing success is to imagine you are the client. You have to have an out-of-body experience and get into the hearts, minds, souls, and shoes of your client.

■ Visualize Your Client

Go to a quiet room, close your eyes, and relax. Now, think about your buyer. I want you to imagine you are driving his or her automobile, cutting his or her lawn, speaking to his or her spouse. I want you to get into the client's head. Feel the client's pain and determine ways in which you can use your product to ease this pain.

Can you see your client? Can you understand his or her thoughts and ideas? If you answered no, then keep trying. For this to work, you must truly understand what is in the mind of your client. It is imperative to understand your client's concerns and issues.

Once you demonstrate genuinely interest in the buyer, it becomes easier to arouse interest. Why? Your questions will be better, and you will be more focused on the buyer's issues and attitudes.

Do not assume that your buyer will be immediately interested. Instead, assume that he is not. You must make the client care. How will you do this? By first asking yourself: How can my product or service be of benefit to the buyer? What use will it provide? How can he or she take advantage of the benefits offered?

Think about these and other questions you will ask the buyer. You must have these at the ready so you are prepared for your call. And don't just think about the questions, be prepared to listen carefully to the buyer's answers.

The goal is to stimulate interest in an action step on the part of the buyer. Know what you want them to do once you have them interested.

To aid in gaining interest, here are some useful techniques:

■ *Question, Question, Question*

As I've pointed out before, sales professionals need to ask pertinent questions. In fact, my rule of thumb is to continue to ask questions until you get to the closing phase of the sales process. In that step, you should be silent to ensure you do not talk your way out of the situation.

Observe the office or physical surroundings of your meeting. What do you see? What artifacts or personal items do you notice in the office or workspace? Do you see family pictures? Do you notice certificates? Diplomas? Do you see children's projects or plants? Look for anything that will pique your curiosity so that you can find common ground. When I worked on Wall Street, as soon as I was escorted into a buyer's office I immediately looked at all four walls, the desk, the floor, and the furniture. I reviewed everything so that I could find common ground and show that I was interested in the client.

For example: I might have walked into a client's office and noticed golf putters, a diploma from a university, pennants from a favorite sports team, family photos, and/or children's projects. Looking for these clues to the client's interests enabled me to find commonality and immediately begin a conversation.

I might say, "I love that pencil box! I have a son and daughter, and I love to display their projects on my desk." Depending on the day and the time available, we might spend several moments discussing children. Not only does this "break the ice," but it also illustrates my interest in the other person. Thus, it enables me to begin asking questions.

I mentioned Norm Strauss, an outstanding sales trainer, in a previous chapter. Norm was a master at answering a question with another question. For example, if a buyer said, "What is the fee for a gallon of paint?" Norm would reply with, "What kind of room are you painting?"

Asked to recommend a color for a room, Norm would ask what the room is used for. This keeps the conversation going and illustrates your interest in resolving problems.

■ *Nothing Happens Without a Benefit*

Remember that the buyer's guiding principle is "What's in it for me?" It is your professional mission to ensure you are speaking solely to the buyer. You could describe a benefit in terms of how *any* buyer could use or enjoy the product or service. Instead, present the benefit to that *particular* buyer in terms of his or her specific needs.

When you tailor benefits to your client, you will automatically arouse interest because you are speaking as if your product or service was developed with them in mind!

■ *Pique Interest*

To help get the prospect interested, you can enable the client to touch, taste, feel, smell, or hear something about the product. The use of the five senses is a plus for any selling presentation. People communicate and learn in different ways, and understanding these will help you create interest.

People learn from what they hear, what they feel, and what they see, but many individuals can learn most effectively from just one of these three types of communication. Surveys indicate that more than 70 percent of adults are most responsive to visual stimuli, 15 percent are most receptive to auditory stimuli, and the remainder are called kinesthetic, or most receptive to tactile stimuli.

By honing in on an person's learning type, you are locking into their interest via the manner in which they communicate, which is to say both the way they like to send information and the way they like to receive it. Again, by taking their perspective, you illustrate your interest in them.

Here are some more details on each of these three learning types:

■ *Visual*

Visual people are those who like to see information. The use of computers, television, flip charts, and diagrams encourage and interest a visual person. They tend to take in everything that they see. They like to have manuals, printed materials, diagrams, illustrations, etc. Visual people also:

■ use words like "I see."

■ want to have a visual demonstration.

■ look up to the ceiling to imagine the product.

■ need pictorial language to understand deep concepts.

Visual communicators like to watch and are bored easily by too much detail. They need time to imagine and draw illustrations. The visual learner will understand more and take more interest in you when you translate print to illustrations or graphs, and provide three-dimensional imagery.

■ *Auditory*

Auditory people are those that like to listen and are intrigued by hearing stories, analogies, and case studies. Auditory people also:

■ talk to themselves while working.

■ are easily distracted by noise.

■ enjoy reading aloud and listening.

■ find writing difficult, but are better at telling.

■ speak in rhythmic patterns.

- learn by listening, and remember what was discussed rather than seen.

- are talkative, and readily engage in lengthy discussions.

Enable an auditory person to "hear" what the service offers. Use words that enable them to hear the "sounds" of the service. You will even hear the auditory person state, "That sounds like a good deal."

You might show the person how your company will perform the service. Or you might explain it as a step-by-step process. Enable an auditory person to take the time to understand your product and allow them to replay what they heard so that they can hear themselves. When they do this, there is a tendency to become more interested because you are playing to their sensibility.

- *Kinesthetic*

Kinesthetic people like to touch and feel; they are very hands on. Perhaps the only available manner in which to gain the interest of a kinesthetic person is to illustrate your service with them "driving."

You will need to have "hands-on" demonstrations and techniques that enable the kinesthetic person to become interested. If you can do this, you may be able to quickly move all the way to closing the sale! Kinesthetic people also:

- learn through touching.

- respond to physical rewards.

- touch people to get their attention.

- stand close when talking to someone.

- learn by manipulating and doing.

- memorize by walking and seeing.

- use their finger as a pointer when reading.

- can't sit still for long periods of time.

As you continue to encourage interest with the kinesthetic communicator, you might find yourself repeating information. Do not be concerned because this is a way they learn and become interested. They might continually pick up the product or service. This is good, because their body language is illustrating their interest and possible intention to purchase.

You might feel as if they are distant and inattentive to you, but they are absorbing your information while becoming more interested in your product. Have patience with them, take your time and do not rush. Enable them to have as much time as they need to become interested.

■ *Draw a Visual*

The brain works in mysterious ways. One of the most fascinating aspects of the brain is how it creates mental pictures. By nature, we are all very visual people. We say pictures are worth a thousand words. If that were really so, imagine how much less we might speak! Regardless, pictures are a great tool for sparking interest.

Words help to place a buyer in a situation with your product or service. The buyer can visualize using your product or service if you frame the picture with the proper words. An example of the mind thinking in pictures is to think of the following words: pencil, policeman, and automobile. Do you have the words or do you have the pictures?

In your head, you probably visualized a yellow pencil, a policeman in uniform, and a picture of your favorite automobile. I never asked you to provide a visual image, just the words. But your mind did not call up the letters P-E-N-C-I-L, did it? With proper pictorial words, you can strive to build interest based on the emotions of the client.

Word pictures are not hard to produce and really do help the buyer synthesize your offer. You might state, "Imagine yourself in a silver Toyota with a blue velvet interior. The car is so quiet that all you hear are the air conditioner and the radio tuned to your favorite music."

You get the picture. I bet that you could see YOURSELF behind the wheel as I provided that description.

There are a few rules for making word pictures work. First, be succinct. The shorter the word picture, the easier it is for the buyer to imagine. Too much information confuses a buyer. Second, tell the buyer what the product does and how the buyer looks using and enjoying the benefits of the product or service.

The best way to arouse desire is to pick up [prospects] mentally and carry them into the future and let them see themselves enjoying what you are trying to sell them. It is an appeal to the heart.

—Percy Whiting

Word pictures are valuable and will enable you to sell in less time and more efficiently. One needs to practice and make the buyer the hero or heroine, but once you have mastered this technique, you can create many buying opportunities.

■ Impact Questions that Gain Interest

In speaking to your clients, try to get them in a frame of mind where they acknowledge some of the pain and displeasure they experience. Give the buyer an opportunity to explain his current condition. Try to get them in the mode where they are dissatisfied and want to talk with you about ways in which your product or service will assist them.

Further, you must begin to ask questions that enable you to play detective. Recall that I wanted you to visualize yourself as the client. As you encourage interest from your client, I want you to begin to think of the following questions and to imagine what replies you might get for each.

■ Do I know why the prospect would buy my service?

■ Do I know what the prospect expects from my service?

■ Do I know how the prospect is planning to use my service?

■ Do I know other ways the prospect could use my service?

■ Do I know how quickly the prospect needs delivery?

■ Have I informed the prospect of the service's limitations as well as its advantages?

■ If a callback is necessary, have I left the prospect with an impression of my service strong enough to overcome a competitor's sales pitch?

These questions will help you establish your client's needs and, more importantly, help you connect with their interests. It is your mission to help them become interested. One of the best lines written comes from one of my favorite books, *The Five Great Rules of Selling*. In this book, author Percy Whiting writes, "Never write 'not interested' on a prospect card. Write instead, 'I failed to interest the prospect.'"

Master the art of interesting the client in your product or service, and you will get to the Finish Line!

"There are two levers for moving men: interest and fear."

—Napoleon Bonaparte

Answer the following questions to determine how you might be able to build interest with the client.

Do I know why the prospect would buy my service?
❏ yes   ❏ no

Do I know what the prospect expects from my service?
❏ yes   ❏ no

Do I know how the prospect is planning to use my service?
❏ yes   ❏ no

Do I know other ways the prospect could use my service?
❏ yes   ❏ no

Have I informed the prospect of the service's limitations as well as its advantages?
❏ yes   ❏ no

What is the value that I provide to the client?

_____

_____

If I do not speak features and benefits but help to resolve an issue what is the issue that I seek to resolve for my client?

_____

_____

Questions to Keep Interest and Establish your Value Proposition to Keep interest flowing:

❏ What is the impending event?

❏ What would happen if you decided to do nothing at this time?

❏ How might this service assist you personally? How can I help with that?

❏ How will this affect performance and productivity?

❏ How can this project assist the bottom line?

❏ What is the intangible impact?

SELLING SCORECARD

List three ideas from this chapter that you will put into immediate use to begin obtaining the results you seek.

☐ *Idea:*

_____

_____

_____

Start Date: _____

Finish Line Date: _____

☐ *Idea:*

_____

_____

_____

Start Date: _____

Finish Line Date: _____

☐ *Idea:*

_____

_____

_____

Start Date: _____

Finish Line Date: _____

EVENT:

INTEREST

chapter 9

P-R-A-C-T-I-*C*-E
Closing

You have been through a good portion of this book and have read much vital information. Now you are ready to learn about the ultimate prize: closing the sale.

Here is a secret you might not know: the top sales killer, and consequently one of the deadliest of all sales sins, is the failure to ask for the order!

I will never forget the day I was in the office of the president of Merrill Lynch. The memory is so vivid I feel I can jump into it as if it were happening now: My colleague and I have been meeting for more than an hour to capture a million dollar software deal. The meeting ends, we get up, and, since my colleague was running the meeting, I let him take the lead in the close. We shake hands, and... we leave.

Yes, we left Merrill Lynch with a $1 million negotiation sitting unfinished on the table. It took months to once again get to the point where we could finally close the deal. Thus, my rule for closing is to go get what you really want—the contract!

■ *ABC's of Closing*

Generally speaking, when it comes to closing, I use the ABC rule: Always Be Closing. During all phases of PRACTICE, you should be asking questions and honing in on the client so that you are always trying to close.

Many sales professionals ask me, "When should I ask for the order?" My answer is, "When you believe the time is right." You will know this from the comfort of the conversation and from the questions raised. However, there are several things you can keep in mind as you go through the selling process.

■ *Buying Signals*

Sales professionals pay attention to both body and vocal language to determine when to close a sale. Body language is most compelling. Typically, buyers will lean forward and appear to get closer to the selling professional. Buyers might also take more notes and ask more questions—these are both buying signs.

As you continue to PRACTICE, you remove the focus from you and your mission and become attentive to the client. Be aware of how the buyer looks and what they sound like. Are you hearing more emotion? Are they asking more questions? The answers to these questions are essential to determining when and how you will move forward.

One of the best techniques for understanding buying signals is simply listening. I know I have said it often in this book, but it's worth saying again in the context of the close: listening is a critical part of what you have to do. You have to listen to questions that the buyer is asking, and if they seem to indicate that the client intends to buy your product or service, waste no time in advancing toward the close. Some of the questions you may get asked include the following:

■ How long will it take to install?

■ Do you offer a warranty on your service?

■ How long until I take delivery?

■ Will somebody help me install it?

■ Do you have a repair department?

■ How long does it take to ship?

■ Suppose I want to buy…?

■ Does it come in blue?

But perhaps the best buying signal of all is when the buyer reaches over and specifically asks you to review the terms of the agreement. The best thing that you can do next is nothing. Your job is simply to pause and to wait. Do not make another point!

Your job is to close the sale. Do not say anything! You're simply to ask for the order as if you are a psychic. You want the close to be a natural part of the conversation. The moment you provide options or give your buyer doubt, they will certainly seize these factors and hold off on finalizing their purchase.

■ Trial Closing

One of the best methods to test the interest of the buyer is to use a trial close. Trial closes are comprised of questions, suggestions, and implications made by the sales professional to determine whether or not the buyer is ready to make an investment. You might want to consider them as feelers.

The difference between a trial close and the buying signals mentioned above is that you are in charge and can control when you use the trial close.

A trial close will help you determine when and how to ask for the order. Simple trial close questions might include, "When might a selection be made for this particular product or service?" It is imperative that you listen for the answer. The buyer's reply will let you know if they are ready to close, or if they are raising an objection. Similar to buying signals, you must listen intently to what the buyer is saying.

I know that it is not easy to ask the questions that get you closer to a sale. A trial close can warm you up so that you are more comfortable taking the leap into the final closing process. Once you have asked the questions repeatedly, you're more comfortable and, consequently, less afraid of asking for what you want! In my experience, a trial close can help determine the buyer's opinion and intentions.

Better trial close questions lead to better answers and inexorably push you and your client nearer to the close.

■ *Twelve Impact Questions*

I began my sales career in 1984. In 1988 I met one of my mentors, Richard. It was not until I started going on sales calls with him that I realized the value, importance, and urgency of a trial close. At that time, Richard suggested that there were seven questions that needed to be asked on each sales call.

In 1993 I added an additional five questions to the mix. I call these 12 questions "Dr. Drew's Dozen." This store of questions will definitely assist you in moving toward the close by getting you the replies that you need. These questions can be asked during the trial close, or they can be asked during the closing portion of your presentation. However, do listen carefully to the replies. The answers will tell you how near you are to closing.

I have found that the secret to success lies in asking all 12 questions, so that you fully understand where the buyer is in the sales process.

1. What is your desired outcome?

2. Who are the players in the decision process?

3. Do you have to make a decision now?

4. How much time do you have to make this decision?

5. What are your options for allocating resources?

6. What feedback or answers do you need to make this decision?

7. What are your preferences or biases about making this decision?

8. How would your boss make this decision?

9. Are the resources to implement this decision in place?

10. What objectives do you hope to meet?

11. Who will sign the check?

12. When will the check be signed?

Additionally you might also add the following:

- If the proposal reflects our last conversation, how soon can we begin?

- Is there anything preventing our working together at this point?

- How quickly are you ready to being once you review the proposal?

- If I get the proposal to you tomorrow, can I call you _____ for approval?

- May I allocate two days early next week to start the focus groups?

- Can we proceed?

One final thought on these 12 impact questions: the theory behind this book takes you through an implied chronological process. While my intention is to give you a logical process, selling always presents different situations. You want logical order, but sometimes there isn't. So, while these questions are listed in the chapter on closing, please feel free to ask them in all phases of your presentation. You need not save them until the very end. Interspersing them throughout your presentation will help to refine your insights into the buyer and his intentions.

■ Ready for Objections

I have what might at first seem to be an odd view of objections: I love them! That is so important I want to repeat it: I love objections!

You might think that is silly, but it is not. Objections simply help you understand where you are in the sales process. Challenging though they are, objections provide valuable touch points to gauge your progress.

By and large, objections are nothing more than concerns and skepticism on the part of the buyer. Objections are the result of indecision, fear, and prior losses. If you have done a good job discussing wants and needs, objections don't get raised as often, but they still appear.

To overcome objections, you must be ready for them. Here are a few major points to keep you on your toes. First, always anticipate that you will receive objections at some point in the process. You should never be surprised when you get one. One of the first things that you need to do when handling an objection is to use a technique that I learned many years ago called the *BIC Principle.*

BIC stands for *Be In Control.* The only way to maintain control during a sales presentation is to constantly listen or ask questions. You should never lose control or seem surprised. Objections are simply a part of the sales process and, more importantly, the closing process. Your ability to remain in control is essential to your success.

A second rule of thumb is to never argue when you receive a sales objection. The buyer is merely seeking to gain more information—it's his or her way of indicating that you have not provided enough data.

Third, objections can be genuine concerns or trivial points. It is incumbent upon you to ask the proper questions to determine whether an objection is genuinely concerning or simply a minor glitch. In my experience, the most common trivial objection is "the price is too high." You must ask more questions to determine genuine objections – in other words, to discern the primary reasons that the buyer considers most valid for not moving forward.

Fourth, too many people want to talk and not listen. Sales professionals can become too focused on trying to close the sale. This can result in the salesperson neglecting to listen to the buyer's objections. The best thing you can do is intently listen to the buyer's reasons for not progressing.

One of the best listening methods is known as "the power of the pause." Quite simply, pause and say nothing. Wait until the buyer speaks. He or she may tell you why the sale is not moving forward, if given the chance. The point is to be patient and let the client tell you what you need to know.

As always, it is imperative that you strive to understand what is going on in the mind of your client. If you can understand what the client is going through, it may be easier for you to ask appropriate questions that will provide the information you need to stifle the client's objections. And the closer you get to your buyer's perspective, the easier it becomes to understand his or her thinking.

Finally, you must address objections one at a time. You will not be able to handle them all at once. Breaking them up into separate components will enable you to handle them more easily. More importantly, after asking a question and getting an affirmative response, you can try to gain commitment. If you elicit several affirmative replies, you might actually get the buyer to move forward. An old adage acknowledges that the whole sometimes can be greater than the sum of its parts. By addressing objections one at a time, it becomes easier to convince the prospective buyer.

When prospective clients raise objections, what they're really saying is that they're not comfortable with the decision for a variety of reasons. Further, they are telling you that they have unresolved questions in their mind. So what's a good sales professional to do? We must simply address their objections. The simplest way to respond to a sales objection is to listen and then follow the rules that I have outlined below.

■ How to Handle Objections

My process for handling objections is to START:

S - Suggest a Time-out

T - Tactfully Deny

A - Admit It

R - Reverse

T - Time to Explain

The most fundamental objective to remember is that when you hear an objection, simply START to reverse it.

First, suggest a time-out so that both parties can consider the offer on the table. As you learned in Kindergarten, stressful situations sometimes require a time-out. There is no reason why this principle cannot be applied in business. Taking a time-out allows for thought and ample consideration of the proposed agreement. It gives buyers an opportunity to consider why they don't want to proceed, and it gives you an opportunity to strategize about how to reverse the buyer's objections.

Split Second Selling

Clearly, a time-out can be very helpful. But don't take too much time —the buyer could decide to walk away.

Second, you can tactfully deny the objection. Even though you may not agree with the buyer's opinion, you must show some sympathy. Treat the buyer with respect, and do not argue. Show him or her that you are concerned about the objection and will do anything you can to understand his or her feelings.

If information is misstated, you can professionally correct it and enable the buyer to save face. Tact is what you need to change an opinion while maintaining your professionalism.

Third, admit it. Sometimes you'll run into objections that are unanswerable. Admit it and move on. If your prices are higher than your competitor's, admit it. If your inventory is lower, admit it. Honesty is the best policy, and your buyer will appreciate your candor and sincerity.

When I cannot overcome an objection, I admit it. I believe that people do not buy a product or service, they buy an experience or a perceived experience. They want a trustworthy and candid salesperson. Your ability to deliver honest answers can place you above and beyond your competition.

For instance, imagine your client wants to buy your product, but he or she feels it is too expensive. The buyer may speak to a lower-priced competitor, but that salesperson seems untrustworthy. Who do you think will get the sale?

Fourth, you can try to reverse the objection. There are many reasons why a buyer might not want to proceed, including fear, procrastination, and loss. If you can, try to identify the reason and turn it into a reason why the buyer should reach a positive purchase decision.

For example, if a client offers an objection such as, "We are happy with your competitor," ask if they are really that happy. If they are, why did they agree to meet with you? With today's competitive market and pressures, extra time is the one thing most people do not have.

That said, there is an obvious reason why the client wanted to meet with you, and it is not because he or she wanted to tell you how contented

107

he is with your competitor. Perhaps fear of change bothers the buyer. Perhaps the buyer wants to learn more about your organization.

Your mission to reverse the objection merely requires that you uncover additional information. The technique of changing an objection into a reason for buying is very effective, and it's not as difficult as you think: listen and frame your reply accordingly.

Give them time to explain their objection. Listen to the buyer's concerns and question their objections. Many sales professionals hear an objection and then are silent. Objections provide the best opportunities to speak.

Listening is key, but this is also the time to really get into a conversation with the buyer. You want to discover the buyer's fears and questions —the reasons for moving forward or not moving forward. Continue to ask questions. Hone in on what the buyer really wants and why he or she is speaking to you. Review your list of product benefits and ensure that you match those benefits with the buyer's needs. As you review this list with the buyer, get him to affirm his interest.

The best defense for objections is to know that you will receive them and plan accordingly. Objections are just hurdles that are part of the sales race. Hurdlers do not go around their obstacles – nor should you!

Sales professionals who anticipate objections are ready to address buyers' concerns. Objections are difficult to overcome with rebuttal, and it is difficult for the buyer to make the decision until he or she is ready. Anticipating objections and having good follow-up questions at the ready will help uncover underlying concerns. Help the prospect put aside fears and confirm confidence in you.

▦ Negotiation Nuggets

A conversation about objections would not be complete without some basic information about negotiation skills. The very first step in negotiation is to begin with what you have in mind. Do not get sidetracked with the numerous things that can occur during negotiations. Listen intently, and then question when the need arises.

Before I begin to describe the various negotiation tactics, I want to share a foundational tool that will assist your negotiations and help you remain flexible. This tool is easy to remember: just think "OOH WHO!"

(Yes, this is another acronym. These mnemonic devices help you remember important concepts during stressful sales calls.)

O—obstacles or objections. Similar to what I mentioned in the previous section, you must anticipate the obstacles and objections that your buyer will present. Lack of knowledge in this area will create animosity on both sides. The earlier you can detect the obstacles, the easier it will be to negotiate.

O—options. Never walk into a negotiation with only one available option. You must have the flexibility of providing several options so you can satisfy both sides. Lack of planning in this area can cause you to lose the sale.

H—have a plan. In order to sell and negotiate, you must have a plan of action. You must know what you're going to say and who you're going to say it to. Planning provides a path to success. Without a plan, you lack focus. The buyer will see this and make it easy to kill the deal.

W—know who you are dealing with. The report section of this book describes in great detail the need to identify with the behavior and personality of your client. Knowing how to identify the four behavioral types is important. Knowing who you are speaking with and how to speak to them is essential to communication success. To gain a deeper knowledge of behavior, review the rapport section.

And to further your knowledge of behavior and personality, visit *www.winningsalesassessment.com*. This Web site will enable you to take your own personal DiSC assessment and understand your personality in relation to others. Once you understand your strengths and abilities, it becomes easier to understand others.

H—how the buyer will negotiate. Understanding from past experience how the buyer negotiates places you at an advantage. Your anticipation of the buyer's aggression or passivity can certainly assist you during a negotiation.

O—own the meeting. I mentioned earlier that you must always be in control. This is true of every sales presentation and every sales negotiation.

In order to negotiate correctly, there are four steps that you need to take: These are planning, communicating, presenting, and bargaining.

■ *Planning*

One of the most important aspects of successful negotiation is planning. Similar to preparing for a sales presentation, you must plan your negotiation. Planning begins with detailing the terms and conditions required. It also includes preparing for resistance from the buyer and identifying your negotiation partner's role in the buying process.

Additionally, planning involves considering how the negotiation will be handled. There are four possible outcomes to any negotiation: These are win-win, win-lose, lose-win, and lose-lose. No party to a negotiation wants to feel like a loser. It is necessary to control the negotiation so that both sides feel as if they have given up little and gained much.

The next stage of planning your negotiation involves defining your goals and objectives. List all the objectives you must negotiate, and their associated issues, in order to reach an agreement. Ensure that you know your deadlines to keep your negotiation on track and meet all your objectives.

The final step is to conduct a *SWOTT* analysis for both sides. Understanding SWOTT enables you to align strengths and weaknesses so that you can see any flaws that might appear during the negotiation. This is a key tactic because the earlier you can outline your weaknesses versus that of the buyer, the earlier you can determine what assistance you might need during the negotiation.

■ *What is a SWOTT Analysis?*

SWOTT is an abbreviation for *Strengths, Weaknesses, Opportunities, Threats* and *Trends*. SWOTT analysis is an important tool for auditing the overall strategic position of a business, its people and its competitiveness in the external environment.

Once key strategic issues have been identified, they feed into business objectives, particularly marketing objectives. SWOTT analysis is used typically as a marketing planning tool because of its generic nature. However, it is also used with other tools such as a *360 Analysis, Force Field Analysis* and *Peer Review.*

There are two implications—the internal environment and external environment. Strengths and weaknesses are internal factors. These include your existing products or personnel, or perhaps your lack of products and personnel.

Opportunities, threats and trends are external factors. For example, an opportunity could be developing distribution channels or markets, or changing a current client's buying behavior. A threat could be a new competitor in an important existing market, or a technological change that makes existing products potentially obsolete. Trends are overall shifts in consumer behavior.

SWOTT analysis should be used as a guide and not an absolute for market or client penetration or issues. However, the administration of a SWOTT analysis does help to graphically depict overall current marketing issues. A quick interpretation, such as SWOTT, can help you make immediate changes so that you sell more efficiently.

While a SWOTT analysis is a subjective assessment for business development, it can be used to assess business decisions such as:

■ changing a supplier

■ new sales distribution

■ strategic planning of a merger

■ a potential partnership

■ creating a new, or deleting, a product or brand

■ new business idea

SWOTT Analysis

Strengths _____

_____

Weakness _____

_____

Opportunities _____

_____

Threats _____

_____

Trends _____

_____

Once you conduct an extensive SWOTT analysis, list any questions and objections that the buyer may raise. Having these questions and objections already listed enables you to be more prepared to close.

Last, but perhaps most importantly, is planning the position you intend to take in the negotiation. There are four methods to negotiate: the first is the opening offer; the second is the best offer; the third is the worst offer; and the last is walking away. You need to consider all four possibilities. Doing so will help you determine what it takes to win the sale and enable you to walk away.

For instance, assume you are purchasing a home listed for $300,000. Your opening offer might be $275,000. Your best offer might be $285,000. The worst offer might be $290,000. And you would walk away if the price reached $295,000. I am only including price in this scenario, but I do recognize that other conditions might affect the course of the negotiation.

■ Communicating

There are two major points related to communication in terms of negotiation—communicating the message and listening to the message.

Just because you speak does not mean the other side hears you. You
must understand that human beings hear many messages throughout
the day. Studies show that we take in almost 2 million bits of information per second. That is an immense amount of data. Since we take in so
much information, our brains do a tremendous amount of filtering based
upon past experiences, interests, values, beliefs, and assumptions. Since
we do this often, we tend to dismiss unimportant information. Do not
assume that all points are heard during negotiation. Speaking does not
mean that your message is getting across.

During communication there is noise. Much of our daily intake of information, mentioned above, consists of noise. Noise is also related to
what we believe we heard versus what we actually heard.

During a typical conversation, most people only process between 5 and
10 percent of the words. Remember, many human beings are primarily oriented towards visual stimuli – they do not remember words, so it
is imperative to ensure that your negotiation tactics stick. You do this
by using effective communication and listening techniques. Before you
negotiate, set an agenda, agree on terminology, set deadlines and action
steps, and, finally, remove any distractions.

In order to keep your communication flowing, paraphrase things that
you've heard. Repeat in your own words what you believe the buyer
said. Ask him to affirm what was stated. Also, avoid using technical or
industry jargon. Buyers may not be familiar with the language, and the
point of negotiation is to make both sides comfortable.

Your body language may betray you. You want your body language to
be neutral in order to hide any signs of arrogance or annoyance. Keep
your speaking pace steady, and do not let your eyes wander from the
client.

Throughout this book I have suggested that you listen to the statements
your client makes. One of the best ways to listen is through questioning.
This was covered in our rapport-building section.

Closed-ended questions allow for only a yes or no reply. Open-ended questions allow dialogue and typically begin with one of the five W's: who, what, when, where, and why (or how). Open-ended questions trigger more enlightening replies and better understanding of issues. They are also used for clarification enabling you to review and examine in more detail what has been previously stated. Finally, they help you focus on particular issues, processes, or procedures.

Another item worth mentioning is caution with certain words. Different words have different connotations. During negotiations it is not possible to always be positive, yet you can eliminate negative feelings by avoiding certain words. These words include: unfortunately, can't, try, might, should, and I don't think. Studies show that these words might elicit negative feelings.

Other words and phrases to avoid include: OK OK, right, and uh-huh. These are known as filler words and typically illustrate a lack of thought and skill in handling an issue.

There is one final group of words to avoid: basically, obviously, bear with me, and let me be honest. All denote lack of sincerity.

The next best communication technique is listening. The best strategy for active listening is note-taking. Writing the issues down helps you understand the buyer. Notes make you listen and keep your mind from wandering. You can also formulate questions from the notes you take. More importantly, notes stop you from interrupting the buyer and imply that everything they say is vital to the negotiation. Notes are a terrific way to build rapport.

■ Presenting

Once you are comfortable with communicating and planning, it is time to present the information. Of all the steps, this is the easiest. My suggestions here are simple: define your time frame, have an agenda, and then begin.

Ensure that both sides understand what is to be discussed. Allow time to ask questions and offer replies. Keeping both sides comfortable and neutral is important.

■ *Bargaining*

We finally arrive at the last step—bargaining. Now it is time to get all negotiation tools working. Your objectives are set, and you know who you are dealing with; now it is time to have a discussion and determine when and how you will develop solutions. I suggest listing all the issues for both you and the buyer. Once discussed, list them in order of priority. Those of highest importance are the last to be discussed; those of lesser importance are those that can be deleted or resolved first.

Know your *BATNA* before you sit down to the table. BATNA stands for *Best Alternative To a Negotiated Agreement*. BATNA is similar to the opening offer, best offer, worst offer and walk away categorizations. You determine what you are willing to settle for and what you can give up. These parameters represent what you and the buyer want and need. And they assist in defining how much you will compromise and when it is not possible to reach an agreement.

As you proceed, know when concessions are necessary. If needed, I suggest beginning with morsels; allowing you to begin the negotiations by giving in on noncritical issues. When possible, try not to offer too many concessions at once. The more you give, the more the buyer expects, giving them the feeling that they have the upper hand. If needed, keep track of concessions so you know how much each side has given.

Finally, you need to know when to push, when to give in, and when to stand your ground. It might be time to push if you see body language that suggests interest. Buyers might ask more questions and begin to lean toward you. They might ask to review the sales agreement. They might even want another product demonstration. When this happens, it might be time to close the sale.

When you have to give in, do so only after making at least one offer. Do not give in too early. Instead, assess the situation and give in only when necessary—when you believe that the buyer will not compromise.

Stand firm after your worst offer is made. You cannot give in further. Walking away must be your final tactic. If you reach this point, take a quick time-out and let both sides consider the issues. Time-outs enable emotions to settle so both sides can think rationally.

Negotiating is not easy. It takes poise, time, patience, and attention to detail. Understanding both sides is crucial to success. Each new negotiation is a learning experience and will make you better. Growth will come from self-evaluation and education.

Evaluate your negotiation performance upon completion. Consider what worked, what didn't work, what you would repeat, and what you should avoid in the future. This process will assist you in making each succeeding negotiation better and increase your chances of closing more sales!

■ *Types of Closing*

As I stated earlier, in my business getting to the Finish Line is all about results. You have come so far and are close to getting your sale. Now it's time to do the thing that most sales professionals fear most—closing. You have invested time and energy asking and answering many questions. You have almost reached the Finish Line!

Welcome to the wonderful world of closing! If you're fearful or uncertain, don't worry. You are about to enjoy the most important aspect of your job. That is getting the contract that you have worked so hard for. Remember, we're all in it for the money. Make no mistake about it, you're not in sales if you don't want to make money. This is perhaps the only profession where the sky is the limit. To create unlimited opportunities, you must follow this simple rule—always be closing. The more often you close, the more money you will make.

One of the techniques offered in another chapter of this book talks about secrets of highly effective sales professionals. One of those secrets is the fact that effective sales professionals are closing most of the time. Such a professional knows not only what to ask but when to ask it. They also know when to listen.

If you continue to talk and do not listen, you could potentially undo your sale. You may have a second chance to make the sale, but you're frequently going to spend a long time working your way back to the point where you're in a position to make the sale again, so why waste your chance now?

It reminds me of the old adage that suggests you only have 30 seconds to make a lasting first impression. In selling, you only have one chance to make a close, and after that your buyer is gone. Know when to close. There is no better opportunity to make money!

Be ready to close at any time. You may have heard that more deals are closed on golf courses that in offices. I do not have statistics on this, but I can tell you that in my many years of selling I have closed sales in restaurants, hotels, taxicabs, and even in the gymnasium. I believe that selling is a nonstop process. If you are a genuine sales professional, you will sell and close whenever and wherever you can. That general principle alone will set you above your competition.

▪ *Don't Leave Home Without It*

I always make it a point to have closing materials with me. This can include, but is not limited to, a presentation and an agreement. Today's technology makes both of these resources all the more portable and accessible.

I am rarely without my personal computer. This allows me to share PowerPoint presentations or even client testimonials. While you might not use them, they often help to create the visual stimuli that most buyers prefer. Although technology is very convenient, I still make it a point to carry printed sales materials.

Always bring with you a professional folio or pad of paper. Nothing has bothered me more than to see sales professionals who attend presentations without the proper tools. Always have more than one pen or pencil so you can take copious notes.

I hear from too many sales professionals that they can remember the most important data. But why take chances and put essential information at risk? If you take notes, not only are you guaranteed to retain important insights, you are providing the buyer with a vivid illustration of how attentive and interested you are in his or her concerns and in doing business with him or her.

Sometimes little things like that can bring you the biggest rewards. Take the time and effort to bring the necessary tools with you. Your ability to use these tools will once again help you rise above the competition.

Depending on your particular market, it may be wise to also carry a calculator. This simple tools allows you to check math, calculate taxes, and check your figures against those of your client. This minute attention to detail will ensure that you do not make human errors and reassure buyers that you want to do right by them.

The most frequently overlooked tool is one that uses the least energy and can relieve the most pain. This tool is not unique, nor does it cost much—it's a simple thank-you card. I send one out after every presentation and seminar I conduct. Nothing creates a more genuine sense of connection than a handwritten card that expresses your appreciation for doing business with the buyer.

Finally, I always prepare specific questions that will allow me to close the sale. Knowing what to say is just as important as knowing when to say it. You want to sound genuine, and you want to sound professional. I suggest memorizing your closing questions so they are second nature to you but you also may want to have them handy in your notes.

■ Closing Techniques

We have examined a variety of helpful tools for closing a sale and have considered both how and when to pursue the close. Now it is time to discuss specific closing techniques. Closing is merely part of the selling process, albeit the the most lucrative part. Consider it the icing on the cake or the reward for having done the job well.

Also, remember that the biggest part of closing is helping the buyer make the purchase decision. There is no one special thing that you need to do. And there are no separate steps that need to be taken. Closing is merely finalizing the process. If you have provided attention, encouraged interest, and helped the buyer understand how your product or service addresses his or her needs, then it is time to help the buyer reach a decision.

As in other stages of the sales process, no one closing technique can be singled out as being better than all others. Knowing several closing techniques will help you be flexible in various situations.

As you're learning the techniques, my advice is to try them one at a time. Using too many new techniques at once will create confusion for both you and the buyer. Once you get comfortable with one technique, continue to use it while adding others as appropriate.

■ *1-2-3 Close*

"The Principle of Three" is one closing method. You offer the buyer three reasons for making the purchase. Go back to your questions and consider the buyer's replies. Bring those into your closing technique.

You might say, "Mr. Buyer, first of all, we do offer blue, which is your first choice; second, the product is immediately available for shipping; and for the next week we can offer you a 5 percent discount." You have stated the three most important reasons for the buyer to make this purchase now, and they should lead the buyer to close the sale.

■ *Affordable Close*

With this technique, you assure people that they can afford what you are selling. This is where a calculator or perhaps a spreadsheet comes in handy. The best approach is to break the investment into small morsels that are easily absorbed by the client's budget.

For example, when I was selling for Dow Jones & Co., we offered major corporations a system worth thousands of dollars. Our sales approach was to point out that the cost of the system was equivalent to the price of buying a bagel and a cup of coffee for all the members of the firm. Since the approach was so simple and easily relatable to everyday expenses, clients quickly signed contracts.

■ *Alternative Close*

In this scenario, you offer a limited set of choices. Recall that when you offer too many choices, the buyer becomes confused. Therefore, the easiest thing you can do is limit the number of choices.

The choices you highlight will depend on what you've heard from the buyer. If the client has mentioned that color and number of seats in a car is important, you might say, "The car comes in blue and yellow, and it is available with two or four seats. Which do you prefer?"

▪ Assumptive Close

In this close, you help the buyer along by acting as if he or she is ready to decide. Give the prospective buyer a visual image to consider. It's as simple as saying, "Imagine, Mr. Buyer, that you're driving down a long and windy mountain road. It is a cloudless, crisp, and cool day. You can feel the wind in your hair as you go around a turn. The radio is playing your favorite song. You can see yourself in our automobile, can't you? You want this car because you're a free spirit, don't you? That's the kind of person we designed this car for."

Using the assumptive close places your buyer in an imagined situation that has him savoring the benefits of your service. Remember that the mind draws pictures, not words. The more you can create in the buyer's mind a vision of how much he or she will enjoy your product or service, the closer you get your buyer to ending the sales process with a resounding "Yes!"

▪ Alternative Technique

This is a simple technique often used in conjunction with the assumptive close. It is important in this technique to have your questions prepared. You want to ask questions that prompt the buyer to compare and contrast alternatives. What you are seeking is for the buyer to lean one way or another based on his or her desires.

Ask simple questions such as: "Which model do you prefer? What color do you like? When do you need shipping? Does a decision need to be made now?"

If you consider these questions, they sound similar to those used in a trial close. You are trying to assess the situation, but by offering alternatives you're moving the buyer toward a final purchase decision, which is your ultimate goal.

▪ Ben Franklin Weighing Close

The Ben Franklin technique is perhaps the oldest closing technique known in the selling profession. As you know, Ben Franklin was not only a wonderful inventor, but one of the wisest men in American history. When confronted with a difficult decision, Franklin would draw a line down the center of a piece of paper. On the left side he would write reasons for a particular decision, and on the right side he wrote reasons against it.

Buyers, like Franklin, are looking at and weighing reasons for and against making a purchase. By starting from a neutral perspective—neither option is right or wrong yet—a buyer can more resolutely move forward toward his or her eventual decision.

Professional salespeople can apply the same principle; draw a line down the middle of a page. On the left, write the reasons for the purchase. On the right, write the reasons against it. Then list all of the reasons the buyer is interested in purchasing your particular product or service.

You want to list as many reasons to support the purchase as possible. Then list the reasons for not moving forward. Creating this list will assist in identifying the client's objections. If you have done a good job and created an appropriate buying environment tailored to your client's needs, then you will have more reasons to move forward. Point this out to the buyer, and ask, "Are you ready to make your investment?"

Ben Franklin's technique not only helps make the sale, but can help keep your client happy after they've made the purchase. The list of positive reinforcements reminds the client of the original reasons for buying the product.

I find for visual people, the writing of the "reasons for" provides an educational process. It enables the buyer to understand in their own mind why they want to proceed. It also sums up much of the sales conversation. This helps reassure the buyer and provides him or her with additional confidence in the final decision.

Think of Sgt. Webb's mantra on the TV show *Dragnet*: "Just the facts, ma'am." The Ben Franklin close helps the buyer stay focused on the facts by summarizing the reasons for making an important buying decision.

■ *Calendar Close*

The purpose of a calendar close is to try to lock the buyer into a particular purchase date in the hope of gaining commitment. This is especially useful for sellers who have inventory. If this is the case, you can tell the potential buyer that the inventory, such as an appliance or computer, will be available for shipment on a specific date.

For example, I recently purchased a personal computer. When I spoke with the sales professional I indicated my interests. He then stated that if I was interested in moving forward, the next scheduled ship date was in six days. The service department required a certain number of days to prepare the machine. The sales professional gave me a choice of dates and my computer was ready for shipment on the date I chose.

▪ Concession Close

Often mistakenly identified as a form of win-win negotiation, which I will describe later in this chapter, the concession close allows the seller to provide a concession in exchange for the close. Some concessions might include hastened delivery, a second choice, special terms, etc. While there are numerous methods used, the major point is to make the close a positive deal for both sides.

▪ Conditional Close

The conditional close links closure to the resolution of the buyer's objections. The seller provides the reasons for the buyer to make the purchase. For instance, a sales professional will ask, "If we eliminate the late payment penalty that concerned you, would you consider buying our service?"

The conditional close points to one very special objection. While I have not covered objections here, it is vital that you recognize the one main issue holding back the buyer. Focusing on the wrong objection will place you further from closing.

▪ Direct Approach Close

If you do not want to sound like the stereotypical salesperson, then I suggest not using the direct approach close. If you are using this close, you had better know your buyer or at least be aggressive enough to be very direct. There is a fine line between being reassuringly confident and annoyingly cocky, and users of the direct approach can sometimes wobble dangerously close to the negative characterization.

The direct approach is generally preferred when you know your buyer well enough that you are not afraid to be direct. There are several instances where I have used this approach with success. A direct approach might begin in the following fashion: "The purpose of my call is to inquire …"

Or your might state, "I'm planning to be in your area on Tuesday, and I wanted to know if you will be available between 1 and 2:30 p.m."

Or you might say, "It appears that your interest in our product is quite keen. I suggest signing the agreement immediately so that we can make our services available to you right away."

Note that there is no beating around the bush. And you must be confident to ask these questions. When you ask such direct questions, consider downplaying your body language so that your confidence does not appear too aggressive.

Additionally, the direct approach requires action. The sales professional must ask a question that requires more than a yes or no reply. Responding to the question must require action on the part of the client.

It is imperative that your questions are succinct so they are heard. My suggestion for you is to have a prepared list of questions to ask so you are comfortable asking them and do not stumble as you do so. This approach requires practice so you are comfortable, consistent, and, more importantly, confident.

The direct approach requires one final qualification: your ability to react quickly to the action the buyer takes in response to your questioning.

■ Demonstration Close

This closing approach requires that you show the buyer your goods and services. The demonstration close uses some of the same techniques you might employ as you convince the buyer to make the purchase decision. I suggest using this technique in combination with another technique, such as the direct approach.

Demonstration suggests the use of one or more of the senses. Have the buyer touch, taste, smell, feel, and/or hear the product. Have them use it at work or home. Years ago, vacuum cleaner salespeople threw dust and dirt on the floor and then asked the potential buyer to use their vacuum to clean up the dirt. Today, it is not uncommon for a buyer to use a computer for a few moments, evaluate software for a specific amount of time, or test drive a car. All of these activities summon the senses into action and move the buyer closer to a decision.

Once the buyer expresses interest as a result of the demonstration, the salesperson must move the buyer to action immediately with the direct approach: "Since you are expressing such interest, are you ready to proceed with a purchase?"

■ Economic Close

The economic close is typically used in the furniture and appliance business. This close seeks to help the buyer pay less for what they get. Typically, an organization or sales professional will offer no payments for one year, a cut in interest rates, or a lower down payment in order to solidify the deal.

Be cautious when using the economic close. I suggest running basic background checks on the buyer to ensure that they can make payments once the bills come due.

■ Emotion Close

The emotion close uses your collection of facts and replies from your sales presentation to help trigger buyer emotion. Listening is essential so you can focus your closing energies based on what you hear. During your sales presentation, the buyer indicates his or her desire for your product. You might hear them say, "I love red," or, "I look great in this…"

Use those thoughts and emotions. Replay them to the buyer in the form of a question. Appeal to their overall sense of desire and need.

■ Empathy Close

Whenever anyone makes a purchase, there is a fear of "buyer's remorse." No one likes to make a poor purchase. Further, there is always skepticism from the buyer. Just like you, a buyer does not want to part with money. You must empathize with the buyer.

Illustrate your sensibility by stating and repeating your understanding of the buyer. You might draw a parallel between yourself and the buyer, possibly mentioning that you have been in a similar situation. Let the buyer know how you handled your emotions and dealt with the situation.

I recall a time when my employer was located on the same floor as a stock brokerage. Occasionally, I would meet some of the stock brokers in the elevator and hear them repeat their closing statements. The brokers would describe how they spoke with the elderly, the handicapped, or the unemployed. While they appeared sympathetic to the buyers, some of the brokers had little integrity regarding their work, and their sympathy was a facade. This is unacceptable for a true sales professional. Honesty is key.

Consider the buyer's predicament and appeal to their emotions. Try to place yourself in the buyer's situation. Buying decisions are difficult for everyone. You and your client share this dilemma, and you can empathize with the client's emotional turmoil.

■ Feel-Felt-Found Close

This closing technique is similar to the empathy close. The purpose is to draw attention to the emotions and sympathies of the buyer. You also can parallel their thoughts and concerns to yourself or to a group of recent buyers. This makes the buyer part of a group, easing feelings of loneliness or isolation.

For instance, you might say, "Many previous buyers feel the same way, and some felt they could not afford the service. However, most of them found that, after making the purchase, they couldn't be happier."

When you begin to use this concept, it may feel awkward. Practice will help. You do not want to sound unprofessional or cheesy, and it may take you some time to master this particular close. When you do, you will see how quickly you will be able to close sales, because of your ability to relate directly to the buyer's wants and needs.

■ *Impending Event Close*

One technique that can be useful in obtaining an immediate buying decision is the impending event close. As the name implies, something is about to happen in the very near future, which makes it sensible for the prospect to buy now rather than wait. This can be as simple as the receipt of a bonus or raise. Or that perhaps an impending acquisition, merger or buyout will move the buyer toward a quick decision.

■ *Minor Point Close*

The minor point close allows you to relate a product benefit to a minor point mentioned by the buyer. Rather than focus on major reasons not to move forward, it may be easier to concentrate on smaller points. Similar to the Ben Franklin close, this particular closing technique can help you provide the buyer with positive reasons for moving forward.

When you identify minor points to focus on, you can use them to outweigh objections against moving forward. This will assist you in closing the deal because the client will contrast the numerous reasons to move ahead against the shorter, if somewhat more significant, list of reasons not to do so. Remember that we're a visual society, so when a buyer sees more reasons for than against, he or she may react automatically in a way that helps close the deal.

■ *Narrative Close*

In this technique, tell a story about a pleased customer. The buyer may relate to the story, which can allay fears and erase objections.

■ *Never-the-Best-Time Close*

Buyers are always looking to stall a sale. Their reasons may include vacations, holidays, budgets, time concerns, etc. The never-the-best-time close works well with customers who strive to delay.

In this closing technique, the seller should be direct and let the buyer know why there is no better time than the present to move forward. You might remind the buyer that your offer is only good for a particular time period. You can try concessions, or you might seek special management approval.

No matter what approach you try, remind the client that you're there to assist and deliver a solution to his or her issues. Your compassion and sensitivity to the situation will make it easier to close the sale. Exhibiting any sense of agitation or aggression will drive your buyer away.

■ Puppy Close

I know most of you reading this book have used puppy-dog eyes when trying to make a sale. You might, for example, try this approach when receiving a traffic ticket. The puppy close involves acting cute to invoke sympathy and a nurturing response. I don't suggest this technique in general, but I do mention it here because it exists as a technique used by some salespeople.

■ Summary Close

The summary close requires you to review with the buyer all the benefits they are going to receive from your product or service. It is necessary to maintain notes about the wants and needs of the buyer so that you can reiterate the benefits of your service and describe how they relate to the buyer's needs.

■ Testimonial Close

The testimonial close attempts to use great references to close your sale. Typically used when working to convince a client to make a purchase decision, the testimonial close afford you an honest opportunity to share others' thoughts and beliefs about the product.

I have always used this technique and believe that using testimonials is one of the best methods for closing a sale. My press kit and closing kit contain testimonials. Buyers want to know who you have done business with and how well you have done.

Testimonials work especially well when the satisfied customer provides a statement of return on investment or other measurement that illustrates the value of your product or service.

■ Ultimatum Close

As its name implies, the ultimatum close presents the buyer with an ultimatum. You may state that if the buyer does not close today, the offer could be withdrawn. Or the buyer may tell you that there is only so much time available to close the deal. This close is related to the direct approach. While you want to be stern when using this technique, you must be prepared to back up your claim.

■ Valuable Customer Close

The valuable customer close involves an offer that makes the buyer feel special. This particular close is used frequently by organizations seeking to upsell existing clientele.

I am a frequent user of this technique. It works very well, because giving concessions to repeat customers helps maintain your client base.

The valuable customer close also creates a great source of referrals. You can use this technique in conjunction with the testimonial close, adding remarks from satisfied customers.

■ Walk Away Close

I have not used this technique often, but it does work. You make an offer, and the client decides not to accept. You then simply walk away.

It is imperative that you know that the client wants and needs your product or service and is aware of the benefits it can provide. If your offer is compelling and well-suited to the client's needs, but he or she still cannot make a decision, then it may be time to walk away.

You will find that, given enough time, the client will call you back to make the sale. I have seen this technique used to sell automobiles, technology, and even training. Make a compelling offer, pause, and then watch sales grow.

"Success and failure both are parts of life, but results always depend on your preparation."

—Danish A. Danial

OBJECTIONS

S - Suggest a Time-out

T - Tactfully Deny

A - Admit It

R - Reverse

T – Time to Explain

My prospect states:

_____

_____

_____

My first reaction:

_____

_____

How to reply using START?

_____

_____

_____

_____

Question to ask after I use START:

_____

_____

_____

_____

CLOSING

REASON FOR MOVING FORWARD	IDEAS AGAINST
_____	_____
_____	_____
_____	_____
_____	_____
_____	_____
_____	_____

NEGOTIATION PLANNER

General Objective _____

Philosophy_____

Issue _____

Strategy	Yours/Theirs
Strengths	Weaknesses
Opportunities	Threats

Tactics _____

Questions	Objections
Evidence	Alternatives

Position Type _____

Opening Offer	Best Offer
Worst Offer	Walk Away Offer

CLOSING

130

SELLING SCORECARD

List three ideas from this chapter that you will put into immediate use to begin obtaining the results you seek.

☐ **Idea:**

_____

_____

_____

Start Date: _____

Finish Line Date: _____

☐ **Idea:**

_____

_____

_____

Start Date: _____

Finish Line Date: _____

☐ **Idea:**

_____

_____

_____

Start Date: _____

Finish Line Date: _____

EVENT:

CLOSING

chapter 10

P-R-A-C-T-I-C-E Evaluation

You've almost completed your journey. PRACTICE is not complete without a discussion about the evaluation of your sales performance. Some sales presentations go well, and others don't. You need to understand what works and what doesn't. In order to PRACTICE, you need to review both your strengths and weaknesses. So the last part of PRACTICE is a comprehensive self-evaluation.

After every sales call, take time to evaluate your performance and understand what occurred. The process is simple and quick. Simply take a moment to ponder what happened.

Ask yourself:

- What went well?
- What didn't go well?
- What will I continue to do?
- What will I avoid doing in the future?
- What skill did I use well?
- What skill do I need to work on?
- Did I make the client comfortable?
- Was the client happy?
- Will the client purchase from me again?
- Can I obtain a referral? Was this an enjoyable experience?

■ *Ups and Downs of Selling*

Selling is a roller-coaster experience, exacerbated by shifting client issues and market volatility. There are days when you will be riding high and days when you will plunge into despair. However, if you treat each day as an educational experience you can enjoy them all!

Selling is an entrepreneurial endeavor that requires passion and professionalism. Your ability to learn from each sales encounter can enable you to love your profession. But it's impossible to learn if you don't reflect on today's issues so that you can enjoy an even better tomorrow.

The self-evaluation process only takes 10 to 15 minutes after each sales call. This should give you enough time to answer the questions listed above and help you build on your successes.

■ *Wow Journal*

One of the ways to learn is to reflect on each experience in a journal. You can create a journal on your computer or in a notebook. I carry a goals/achievements record and a journal with me each day.

On my goals sheet, I record my personal and professional achievements, highlighting important information. I then write a summary in my Wow Journal. Examples of achievements include winning contracts, obtaining new clients, and participating in special family events.

You might say, "I have a good memory, and I'm too busy to write all this down." Perhaps you are. But there are two things you should consider: we live in a very negative society, and there are days that you may feel depressed. That's when your Wow Journal is invaluable.

I keep my journals and goal/achievements sheets and review them at the end of every quarter. Reviewing this important information makes me feel great. It illustrates that, while I may be caught up in a difficult moment, there are numerous things to be thankful for. It shows me that I have contributed much to my personal and professional world and helps me change my negative perspective. Reviewing this positive information also releases new energy, which allows me to perform at maximum capacity.

■ Evaluate Often

I suggest you review your goals and current situation at least once a month. Take 15 minutes away from the office to review your goals from the previous month and for the upcoming month. Understand what is working for you and what areas call for more research and evaluation. You might even list your *Best Skills Learned* and identify areas for improvement.

Goals	Date

Important Calls	Date

Business to Do	Date

Chores and Personal Items	Date

Best Result Date: _____

New Habit: _____

Notes: _____

To obtain a free copy of the Goal Planning Sheet
send an email to **info@gettingtothefinishline.com**
Reference Code: Goal Sheet

■ *Rewarding Yourself*

You have worked hard to achieve your goals. And the most important person to applaud your success is you! Reward yourself for a job well done. We are good at beating ourselves up, and we often forget to congratulate ourselves. Rewards are a great way to stimulate or maintain motivation.

Instead of focusing on your shortcomings, pay attention to your accomplishments and talents. Even the smallest reward can work psychological wonders as you travel from milestone to milestone. Some examples of rewarding activities include:

■ Meditate

■ Go for a walk, run, or hike

■ Ride a bicycle, scooter, or motorcycle (but only with a helmet)

■ Go to a museum, movie, or park

■ Call a friend

■ Enjoy a cup of coffee or tea

■ Exercise

■ Get a massage

There are numerous things that you can do to reward yourself. And there are numerous excuses for not doing them. Reward yourself for something today. You'll be glad you did!

■ *Rewarding Clients*

Once you reward yourself, remember to reward your clients. Satisfied customers are a source of referrals and future sales commissions. Typically, a client who has a good experience will provide information about that experience to another person. On the other hand, a client who has a bad experience will provide information about that experience to six or more people. A simple thank you note honors your client's contribution to your success.

There is a famous line by Dale Carnegie: "Let's remember that the only way to find happiness is not to expect gratitude—but to give for the joy of giving." This is so true! Give your heart and soul to your clients and demonstrate your appreciation for their continued patronage. Illustrate the value of the relationship. Keep rewarding them and you'll keep your clients for life!

One of the ways that you can remain in contact with clients is by using the 25 to 30 to 50 Rule. Make a list of your top 25 clients who can provide you with future sales or sales leads. This is your circle of influence. It is crucial to maintain contact with this group. Remember, 20 percent of your customers or referral network provides 80 percent of your income.

Contact your circle of influence at least once every 30 days. It does not matter if you call, email or write a note. Just remain in touch so that you are remembered. Clients are busy, and your competitors are trying to keep their attention, too! Do your part, and do something memorable!

At least once every 90 days, you might send your top clients a small gift. This does not mean you are "buying" your clients. The price of gratitude need not be high. Spend no more than $50 per client. Gift cards, luncheons, wine, chocolate, or gourmet coffee are excellent thank-you gifts.

■ Education Often

Sales is unlike most other professions. It takes constant practice and continuing education. A hearty appetite for learning is a must. Those who are informed and educated will fare much better than the competition.

The hallmark of a good sales professional is the ability to work smarter, not harder. Look for books, tapes, and CD's that resonate with you and teach these important lessons.

Over the years, I've developed a list of favorite authors and speakers. I encourage you to discover them for yourself and follow their advice. Education can never be depleted. Check out these exceptional authors:

■ Dale Carnegie

■ Tony Robbins

■ Norman Vincent Peale

■ Og Mandino

■ Zig Ziglar

■ Brian Tracey

■ Les Brown

■ Jack Canfield

You can listen to audiobooks during your commute or daily workout. The point is to commit to the principle of lifelong learning and savor tomorrow's success!

"You don't need fancy highbrow traditions or money to really learn. You just need people with the desire to better themselves."

—Adam Cooper and Bill Collage

What recent accomplishments have I had?

_____
_____

What recent selling shortcomings have I experienced?

_____
_____

What occurred?

_____
_____

How might I have changed the outcome?

_____
_____

What development do I need to assist with these issues?

_____
_____

Where can I gain the assistance?

_____
_____

Who can I get to mentor me?

_____
_____

When will I do this?

_____
_____

When should I see a result?

_____
_____

EVALUATION

SELLING SCORECARD

List three ideas from this chapter that you will put into immediate use to begin obtaining the results you seek.

☐ *Idea:*

_____

_____

_____

Start Date: _____

Finish Line Date: _____

☐ *Idea:*

_____

_____

_____

Start Date: _____

Finish Line Date: _____

☐ *Idea:*

_____

_____

_____

Start Date: _____

Finish Line Date: _____

EVENT:

EVALUATION

PART 2:

Game
Day

chapter 11

Proposals That Work

O ne of the most powerful tools that you have as sales professional is the proposal. This document is vital to your success, because it summarizes discussions with potential clients and outlines future action steps.

Do not begin a conversation with a potential client by presenting a proposal. Instead, use the proposal to summarize initial discussions and outline future plans, so there is no disagreement moving forward.

Well-written proposals are key to your success. The proposal process helps avoid obstacles and address challenges that you may face while enabling both sides to agree on basic concepts. In addition, proposals encourage action and initiate a contractual relationship with a client.

Before you write a proposal, you must understand the client's wants and needs, dominant buying motive, and value that your product can provide. As you have probably gathered, a large portion of this book is dedicated to building relationships and value-based selling. Proposals help clarify your role as you seek to create those relationships and bring value to your clients' lives.

For the past 25 years, I have used the same format for proposals. It is very simple, and can help your profits rise to new heights. The components of a successful proposal for both tangible and intangible products and services are:

■ Situation Summary

■ Objectives

- Value
- Measure of Success
- Methodology
- Timing and Scope of the Work
- Joint Accountabilities
- Compensation
- Next Steps

The First Hurdle

Before you put pen to paper, it is necessary to meet with the client to determine his or her needs. Do not draft a proposal based on an email or voice-mail message.

For you to become the leader in your field, you must stand head and shoulders above everyone else. You must illustrate that you do things that no other sales professional will do. Regularly meeting with the client is one example.

Your job is not to pursue a commission but rather to assist the client. Once you've reached a mutual, conceptual understanding and the client has agreed to move ahead, you may prepare a formal proposal.

Situation Summary

The first step is to summarize your initial discussions. This is vital, as it illustrates to the client that you have been listening and asking the right questions. The situation summary helps to qualify your conversations and itemize those items that you and the prospective client agree on.

Your job here is not to propose anything new or to sell anything. Your only mission is to write a simple summary. When written correctly, you will illustrate your professionalism by summarizing points that were trivialized or forgotten by the client. Your willingness to listen and review this information shows the client that you want to help.

This section may be written in prose or bullet points. Regardless of format, make sure this opening section illustrates that you and the client are on the same page.

▧ *Objectives*

Objectives are vital to your success. They provide the client with an indication of how you will resolve their pain. Objectives illustrate what you will do in a certain period of time.

You need to ensure that these objectives are complete thoughts. You are not presenting new information, but you are documenting your intentions regarding what you will provide and what the client will gain by using your product or service.

My advice here is to be specific yet concise. One of the best ways to introduce objectives is to outline them. This will ensure clarity while getting to the heart of the matter. Typically, you should list three to six objectives.

Each project is different, but you want to suggest at least three ideas that will instigate change. Any fewer may cause a client to be concerned about value. And more than six will appear too cumbersome and complex.

▧ *Value*

The value section of your proposal will outline the client's wants and needs. This presents an opportunity to reinforce what you bring to the table and describe how your product or service provides value.

Value is difficult to measure. Every client has a different situation and pain threshold. You must show how your product will alleviate the client's pain. For example, value might be measured by anticipated increases in productivity or profit.

Below is an example that illustrates how your proposal might define value:

> *By providing the programs offered in this proposal, Company XYZ can expect an estimated 30 percent increase in productivity due to improved staff communication, leadership, and satisfaction. Intra-office bickering, miscommunication, and tension will subside, and the company will enjoy increased profits as a result of improved productivity and employee participation.*

In today's competitive and pressure-laden world, clients seek immediate, measurable results. In fact, my friend and colleague, Fred Gleeck, says, "Measurement eliminates argument." This is so true. And clients agree.

In order to illustrate value, vision, purpose, and direction – and ultimately get a client signature on your proposal – inform the client in quantifiable terms how your product or service will provide value.

■ *Measure of Success*

This section is critical to the success of your project. While it may appear that this section pertains to value, it really illustrates what changes a client is likely to notice. As a consultant, it is your job to become a futurist and describe what will happen at the end of the project.

The mission of this section is to propose answers to important questions, such as:

■ What does office morale look like?

■ How does communication flow?

■ What percentage of customers are satisfied?

■ Do managers communicate employee expectations?

■ When is there a noticeable measurement for increased workflow?

As the proposal writer, you will be making suggestions related to the objectives and values that you propose. You have two critical roles: to enable the client to envision success and to help the client visualize you as an integral part of that success.

When you devote time and energy to this section, you will immediately separate your organization from the remainder of the pack. How so? By enabling the client to imagine how success will feel, taste, sound, smell, and look.

This is a unique aspect of your proposal—many sales proposals lack this important section. Remind yourself to answer the client's primary question: "What's in it for me?" By providing detailed and colorful prose that answers that question, the client will begin to trust you as a business associate and friend.

▓ *Methodology*

This section explains exactly what you are going to do, when you are going to do it, and how long it will take. The objective is to be clear, specific, and accurate.

You are outlining specific objectives here, and you must be clear about what you will deliver. If the project is to be delivered in stages, mention this here. If specialized equipment or analysis is required, mention this too.

While providing a written agenda of your objectives, do not provide too much information. It is possible that your competitor will learn what your proposal contains. Clients sometimes talk with many salespeople. Thus, you need to provide content that suggests you will solve your client's problems without enabling your client to share critical information with competitors in order to seek a better deal.

For example, when proposing a sales training program, I state in the methodology section that I will conduct a needs assessment of at least 10 employees; I provide a sample training agenda; and I propose a 30-day, post-training follow-up. I do not, however, provide specific assessment or follow-up questions.

▓ *Timing and Scope of the Work*

You should be very clear on the length of time you will spend on the client's account. While based on past experience, estimate enough time that you will be adequately compensated for your tireless efforts on the client's behalf.

Most proposals are about 90 percent accurate in this regard. Include a statement that indicates "additional time is billed on a per diem basis."

▓ *Joint Accountabilities*

This is my favorite section of the proposal. It details responsibilities and accountablity for you and the client.

You may want to reiterate some of the proposed timeline from the previous section in order to clarify that the client must provide certain information in order for you to proceed in a timely manner.

You may work on the premise, "The client is always right," but joint accountability makes both parties responsible for success.

■ *Compensation*

Now it is time to estimate total costs. Do not use a lot of fancy phrases here. Simply estimate the project cost based on your methods, time and joint accountability, as describes in the proposal's previous sections.

Specify your rate per day, month, hour, project, or phase. If your rate is based on personnel or other costs, specify that. Also specify any discount you are offering.

I recommend that you require an initial deposit to begin the project with the balance billed in phases based on work completed. Also include an expense statement. If your project includes travel, written materials, or outside resources, include a statement of associated fees. You are in this to make money, so cover all your bases and keep what is yours.

■ *Next Steps*

Never end a proposal without an action plan. Define what occurs after the acceptance of the contract.

An example of next steps might include the following:

> *Upon agreement, a deposit in the amount of $XXX is required, and the project will begin within 15 days.*

> *I will call you within the next five business days to discuss this information and provide you with additional details.*

> *If, after your review, you have any questions or comments, please call me at xxx-xxx-xxxx.*

Ensure success by including each section, take your time, and consider everything before putting pen to paper. With practice, items will fall into place, and you will see more positive results.

> *"Excellence is in the details. Give attention to the details and excellence will come."*
>
> —Perry Paxton

SELLING SCORECARD

List three ideas from this chapter that you will put into immediate use to begin obtaining the results you seek.

☐ *Idea:*

_____

_____

_____

Start Date: _____

Finish Line Date: _____

☐ *Idea:*

_____

_____

_____

Start Date: _____

Finish Line Date: _____

☐ *Idea:*

_____

_____

_____

Start Date: _____

Finish Line Date: _____

EVENT:

PROPOSALS

chapter 12

Effective Sales Presentations

Most people are afraid of public speaking. Sales professionals, however, are required to make frequent presentations.

There are ways to overcome the fear of public speaking. Coincidentally, even professional speakers get nervous. The secret is to know the audience, the content, and the venue so well that you can concentrate on one thing— the message.

In order to become more comfortable with public speaking, you must understand your fear. Remember, FEAR is nothing more than False Experiences Appearing Real. You amplify your fear by focusing on it. Instead, use your fear. Make it work for you. Accomplished presenters convert nervous energy into positive energy.

Some tactics speakers use to overcome their fear include:

- Be well-prepared before speaking to a group.
- Practice your speech.
- Have a backup, in case you forget what you want to say.
- Don't be afraid of your audience.
- Relax just before you speak.

I will discuss these one at a time to assist you in understanding how to turn fear into a positive force.

■ Be Well-Prepared

Like many people, you may be afraid you will forget what you want to say when facing a group of people. Remember, the content should be extremely familiar to you. After all, you outlined the presentation, wrote it, and practiced it. Be confident that it is virtually impossible to forget everything.

Second, and perhaps most important, no one likes to see you fail. I have spoken in front of thousands of people and I know that no audience wants me to fail. While audience members might not agree on the concepts and ideas presented, I have never had anyone tell me that I was unprepared, lacking materials, or incomprehensible. Remember, your audience wants to learn and is looking for new ideas.

Finally, you can use notes to remember key points, ideas, and quotations. You might need a price list, testimonial, or some other piece of information. No matter how well you know the material, always prepare supporting information.

■ Practice Your Speech

One of the best ways to overcome fear is to prepare for every presentation. First, arrive early. Second, mingle with the audience prior to the presentation so that you begin to feel more comfortable with the people around you. Third, and most important, practice your presentation, but don't attempt to memorize it word-for-word. You want to ensure that the presentation sounds natural.

You may want to prepare index cards with notes and bulleted text to prompt you, if needed.

■ Have a Backup

During my sales career, there have been several times when my presentation did not go as planned. For instance, a computer-generated graphic may fail to work on the projector. This is why it's important to create a backup of every presentation.

It's a good idea to have both electronic and printed copies of your presentation. You may also email an advance copy of the slides or handouts to the meeting planner.

■ *Self-Talk*

I'm a big advocate of self-talk and have used it for many years. It is a wonderful technique for dissipating nervousness and self-doubt.

I have discussed visualization in detail earlier in this book. It is useful in almost all phases of the sales process, including as an aid to presentation preparation. Self-talk is an adjunct to this technique.

To practice visualization in relation to presentation preparation, retreat to a quiet room, relax, and visualize your presentation. Visualize yourself on stage and see the audience listening.

Once you have visualized the experience, tell yourself, "I will give a good presentation. I will do well. I will succeed. I will give the best presentation of my life!"

Self-talk involves affirming the positive outcomes you desire. Self-talk can help you overcome fear and become more positive.

Positive self-talk overrides fear by building confidence. You can use self-talk to address a problem, situation, or potential need. Negative self-talk, on the other hand, magnifies fears, promotes self-doubt, and instills a defeatist attitude. By thinking positively and focusing on positive outcomes, you develop a can-do attitude and become a more powerful presenter.

■ *Reduce Fear of Audience*

One of the most powerful techniques you can use to overcome fear of your the audience is to simply forget about them. Focus instead on your content. Your mission is not to concentrate on the audience; your mission is to concentrate on your message and on your delivery. You can control your delivery, you can control the message, but you cannot control the audience. Focus on what you can control.

One critical element of presentation preparation is analyzing your audience. Good audience analysis requires going beyond your initial assumptions and gathering information about the people who will be affected by your presentation.

Much of what you need to know is covered by three specific questions:

■ Who are they?

■ What do they expect?

■ What do you want them to do at the end of the presentation?

■ Who Are They?

The first question encourages you to find out as much as you can about the audience, including demographic and psychographic information. Also, you can ask the meeting planner for attendees' names and titles.

Although most of your analysis will occur before your talk, you must keep collecting information even during the presentation. It is helpful to meet audience members prior to the presentation. You can gauge their interest level through body language and tone of voice. You also may gather some useful information that can be helpful to insert into the presentation itself.

You might also research the relationships between audience attendees. Indentify key decision-makers, influences, and even check writers.

■ What Do They Expect?

You must think about your audience's background and information needs. Think of our old standard, "What's in it for me?" By answering this question, you focus on the needs of the participants and do not waste their time.

By considering audience members' needs you also affirm their expectations and ensure that you do not reiterate information. You do not want to bore the audience with idle facts and trivial data.

You want to remember that the audience's time is valuable. Therefore, create an agenda and stick to it. When possible, involve audience members or facilitate a group discussion. Clearly, the audience expects a presentation that is informed, clear, and purposeful.

Audience members generally exhibit one of four general personality types, which are discussed below. Once you know the overall makeup of your audience, it's important for you to consider individual personalities. By incorporating both audience and individual analyses, you leave nothing to chance.

During your presentation, maintain your focus on the audience as a whole, not on any one individual. However, by understanding individual personalities, wants, needs, strengths, and expectations, you will develop a more personalized presentation that will make you more credible.

■ *Personality Types*

There are four general personality types present in any audience. By understanding each, you can tailor your presentation for maximum effect. In this section, I will describe each of the four personality types. For additional information, visit *www.winningsalesassessment.com* for a complete explanation and personal DiSC assessment.

We all grew up with the understanding that we are to follow the Golden Rule: Do unto others as you would have them do unto you. However, this is not an effective sales method. As salespeople, we must focus on our client, not on ourselves.

Instead, use the *Platinum Rule.* Developed by Tony Alessandra, the Platinum Rule helps you understand how to communicate more effectively with others. The Platinum Rule states, "Do unto others as they expect to be communicated to." In other words, concentrate on the client's needs. By focusing on your audience and by gearing your communication to their desires, you will have a more focused and motivated presentation.

The following diagram shows the four personality types that form the basis for motivation and communication:

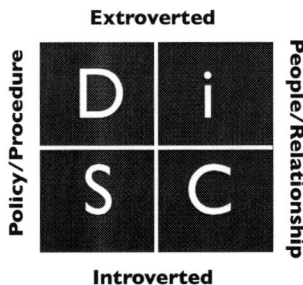

As we explored earlier in this book, these personality types comprise the DiSC profile.

■ Dominant/Dictator

When you walk into a room, you will instantly recognize a Dominant personality. This person wants to run the show. Dominants want results, performance, and profits.

Feelings are not important to Dominants. They know what they want, and they will go to extremes to get it. Dominants ask many questions and want specific answers. They want control. When speaking to Dominants, you must remain focused and retain control.

Dominants also are sticklers for policy and procedure. They respond well to an agenda with specific time frames and answers with specific data.

■ Influencer/Socializer

The Influencer is perhaps your greatest ally. He wants to be social, loves conversation, and enjoys the spotlight. Influencers may interrupt your presentation by speaking to others and asking questions.

It is not uncommon for an Influencer to arrive late, make jokes, and draw attention to himself. However, Influencers are the easiest personality type to get along with. Additionally, the Influencer is driven by basic instincts. They act and respond to others so that they can enhance their security and well-being.

■ Conscientious/Analyst

Conscientious/Analysts are needs-driven. This particular group focuses on deadlines and results. At one time or another, most of us complain about this group because we believe they are too analytical.

The Conscientious/Analyst is very detail-oriented. Therefore, you must be quite specific during your presentation. Keep materials relevant, concise, and oriented to personal interest when addressing this particular audience. Failure to do so will create a dispassionate, disinterested audience, and result in a poor presentation.

■ *Steadiness/Comforter*

Steadiness/Comforters are the most fun. Although introverted and shy during meetings, they love to listen and be part of the crowd. They're cheering for you just as much as they're cheering for everyone else. They want everyone to succeed.

One final note before we end our discussion on audience expectations. In addition to understanding the audience's wants and needs, strive to understand their underlying personal and professional desires.

Remember, an audience might *need* a product or service but not *want* it. For example, an organization might need to obtain consultants to provide annual performance reviews, but it may not want to obtain theose service for fear of cost, time, etc.

Conversely, an organization may *want* to purchase new computers for the office, however, due to budget and space constraints it may not *need* the computers at this time. These are important factors to understand.

When you're making a presentation, there will be things that your audience needs to know and other things that they want to know. As a presenter, it is your job to determine what the audience wants to know versus what they need to know. I suggest you use a needs assessment when collecting your audience information so that this content addresses their wants and needs. And do not forget to include the possible benefits associated with each of those wants and needs.

Attendees will also have personal and professional reasons for attending your presentation. In our computer example, if the office manager can secure computer equipment at a discount, the company may purchase quickly. The professional reason for attending the presentation is to potentially buy computers. The personal reason for obtaining the computers is to increase productivity and gain kudos for saving the company money.

Wants and Needs Worksheet

Description	Wants	Needs	WIIFM
Personal			
Professional			

■ What Do You Want Them To Do?

Sales professionals must take the lead and exert control by telling others what to do. If you want your attendees to take action after your presentation, you must tell them. Whether it is signing a contract, scheduling a follow-up meeting, or writing a report, be specific.

To that end, it is your job to tell participants exactly what you want them to do. Keep it simple, be concise, and write it down. At the end of the meeting, you must be able to summarize and recall all expectations and discussions that have occurred in the wake of your presentation. Include specific objectives, as described in the proposal chapter.

Now that you understand the importance of the audience and know how to overcome your fear of public speaking, it's time to put the presentation together. This section will help you determine how to get all of your thoughts into one coherent presentation.

■ Presentation Structure

To be truly effective, a presentation must be more than the sum of its parts. Achieving that means having the right parts in the right order. Whatever the specific objective of your presentation, strong preparation and proper organization are your keys to success.

Whether you're introducing a new product to a group of prospective customers, presenting a new departmental strategy to management, or just welcoming the troops to the annual office party, your effectiveness is enhanced by a well-organized presentation.

There is a rule of thumb for a clear presentation; "Tell them what you are going to tell them. Tell them. Tell them what you told them." Every presentation should follow this structure.

The outline below will help you organize your thoughts and develop your presentation so that you can cut portions if time runs short, or linking ideas in order to elaborate. (For further help, see the Presentation Planning Guide in Part 5: The Locker Room on page 234.)

The first thing you need to address is your topic. Then you must outline objectives to support the topic. Finally, you want to provide the agenda so that people anticipate the time and level of detail involved.

Presentation Topic: _____

Goals and Objectives: 1._____

2._____

3._____

Agenda for Today: 1._____

2._____

3._____

Once you have completed your agenda, develop your key points. Write down your most compelling point, which will serve as your opening, support it in the body of the presentation, and create a rational conclusion that summarizes the information and moves the listeners to the next logical step.

Transitions are an important means of keeping the presentation fluid and allowing each topic or concept to flow smoothly.

If you have given a presentation to a group of prospective clients your final call to action might be, "Will you buy this?" Take some time to develop this aspect of the presentation, as you want to be direct yet not overly aggressive.

■ *Preparation and Planning*

Once you have finished preparing your presentation, rehearse it. Practice makes for a much better presentation.

- Review your presentation outline. This will ensure that your transitions, topics, and summary all coincide and enable the presentation to flow.

- Memorize key points.

- Record your presentation with the trial crowd.

- Be comfortable with your transitions, summary, and call to action.

- Practice with your visual aids.

- Visualize yourself giving a presentation.

- Ask someone to critique your presentation by reviewing your topic development, slides, or rehearsal.

Clearly, the more you practice, the better you feel. Also, the more comfortable you are with the presentation, the better your delivery.

■ *Presentation Delivery*

There are several ways to deliver a presentation. As previously mentioned, you want to be relaxed but to appear comfortable in front of the group follow a few time-tested techniques.

Stand in one particular place. Do not move around too much, pace, or make erratic movements. These nonverbal elements affect your delivery. Your hand should rest comfortably at your side—not on your hip. And don't cross your arms, as this may make you look defensive. Stand up straight, but maintain a relaxed posture.

In addition to body language, be aware of your facial expressions and vocal traits. Look straight at the audience with a friendly expression, and speak in an audible tone without shouting. Remember to *PIVT:* pay attention to your *Pitch, Inflection, Volume,* and *Tone.*

The best speaking location is at the front of the room, either in front of or behind a table. Many presenters stand behind a lectern, but this can make them appear inaccessible and stiff.

While many presenters utilize multimedia devices, it is imperative to face the audience and avoid reading what's on the screen. By reading the screen, the presenter implies that the audience is incapable of reading the information themselves and gives an impression of being unprepared. Instead, include keywords on your slides. These will keep you on track while allowing you to provide important supporting details.

If your presentation includes visual aids, be prepared for technical difficulties. The more technical props you rely on, the more risk of technical failure. Always have a Plan B.

Also, there is no need to use animation, intense graphics, or a variety of different fonts when preparing slides. The easier your presentation is on the eyes, the better. Straightforward information makes for a powerful presentation.

If a presentation is content-driven and no humor is necessary, then do not make jokes. However, if there are times when you feel it is appropriate to share a humorous anecdote, please do so. Humor builds rapport and can add spice to your presentation.

■ *Thinking on Your Feet*

One of the most important elements of giving a presentation is being in control at all times. You might have an excellent presentation prepared, but it is how you are perceived that matters most. The audience must believe and trust you.

One of the first things to do in order to gain immediate control is to let the audience know what your background and capabilities are. You might ask somebody to introduce you to help familiarize the audience with your credentials.

Something I like to do during my presentations is ask questions of the audience. This provides the participants with an opportunity to interact while allowing me to establish rapport and trust.

There will be times during your presentation when you need to think on your feet. Interruptions, questions, rude remarks, and even hostile listeners may present a challenge. Simply deal with these in a professional manner without becoming defensive.

You may want to set some ground rules before your presentation begins in order to help minimize interruptions.

One way to deal with rude or hostile audience members is to simply ignore them. On the other hand, if you can address their concern immediately, you may eliminate further outbursts. An assertive response to a rude audience comment may create a power struggle, which is to be avoided at all costs. However, in some cases, it throws the audience member off-balance to ask him or her to clarify the point. Just don't let the individual get carried away—it is your responsibility to control the length of the presentation.

If you do some homework before the presentation and understand the audience's personalities, you may be able to communicate with an interrupter in the most effective manner for his or her personality type. This is one reason why DiSC and other personality assessments are so helpful and important.

You reaction to interruptions will influence the audience's perception of you. Hence, proper planning and preparation for these instances are critical.

■ Bringing the Presentation to a Close

We've covered the basic elements of delivering a good presentation. The hard part is over. Now it is time to concentrate on action steps and follow-up activities.

The closing remarks of your presentation are extremely important. Just like when you close a sale, you should ask participants to do something. You want your audience to understand the information you provided and enthusiastically commit to take action based on what they've heard.

Some presenters like to invite audience questions at the end of the presentation. Questions and answers help to clarify and expand upon points of special interest. This type of closing is especially useful after a lengthy presentation.

If you are presenting a tangible product, you may invite audience members to come forward and examine the product. This provides them with a memorable sensory experience. If you are concerned about the product being handled by so many people, you can demonstrate the product as your closing illustration.

A more creative, fun, and unique closing method involves an audience-participation quiz. Individuals who can answer questions about the presentation win prizes. Simply tossing chocolates to the correct responder is a fun way to encourage participation and helps cement the main concepts in people's minds. Of course, don't attempt this in a formal business setting. Use it with more informal group presentations.

■ Final Thoughts

Public presentations need not be frightening. The information provided in this chapter is meant to give you guidance so that your presentations have more meaning and polish. Proper preparation and an understanding of your audience will help you create winning presentations.

> *"There are no uninteresting things,*
> *only uninteresting people."*
> —Gilbert Keith Chesterton

SELLING SCORECARD

List three ideas from this chapter that you will put into immediate use to begin obtaining the results you seek.

☐ *Idea:*

_____

_____

_____

Start Date: _____

Finish Line Date: _____

☐ *Idea:*

_____

_____

_____

Start Date: _____

Finish Line Date: _____

☐ *Idea:*

_____

_____

_____

Start Date: _____

Finish Line Date: _____

EVENT:

PRESENTATIONS

chapter 13

Peak Sales Performance

Peak sales performers are very similar to professional athletes – they love the thrill of victory and abhor the agony of defeat. Peak sales performers thwart competitive threats, service their customers well, and exceed revenue expectations.

What separates the peak performer from the rest of the pack? Peak performers have a passion for selling.

Enthusiastic, energized salespeople are naturally more successful. Peak performers also love sales and believe in the value of their product or service. Their conviction is evident by the obvious enjoyment they take in their work, which clearly engages their clients.

Another important attribute of peak sales performers is the ability to be self-motivated. Those who understand how to operate without much direction are typically the most successful.

■ CEOs of Selling

In many cases, these peak sales performers view their territory as a Small Business Unit. They understand how to make profit, accommodate loss, budget, and see a project from start to finish. They think like entrepreneurs.

Peak performers also are proud of their company and products. Customers love to purchase from people who are excited, involved, and interested in achieving long-term success. Buyers also want to be educated about the products they intend to purchase. Thus, a well-informed, knowledgeable sales professional has an edge over the competition.

Organization is another key trait of peak performers. Great salespeople are extremely goal-oriented and are good time managers. Harvey McKay, author of "Swim with the Sharks," once stated that "goals are nothing more than dreams with a time frame." Yet for peak sales performers, these dreams regularly become reality because they instinctively know how many appointments to make in order to exceed their sales quota. Their sales goals drive them to succeed, and the monetary rewards follow.

These peak performers typically operate in standard blocks of time: about 65 percent is spent with customers, and the remainder is used for travel, reports, follow-up, and paperwork. Further, peak performers keep working until they meet their objectives, even if that means putting in more than 40 hours a week. They know that successful sales is a nonstop endeavor.

Based on all these attributes, it is not surprising to learn that peak sales performers do not procrastinate. The delegate when appropriate and spend their time wisely in order to achieve results. You will not see them chatting at the water cooler, talking to friends on the telephone, or wasting time with nonvital administrative tasks.

▪ Business Planning

To help them stay on track, peak sales performers have a clear business plan. They develop written goals and objectives, carefully plan sales calls, perform strategic analysis of their territory, and research their potential customers. This serves two purposes: It provides a comprehensive road map to follow in pursuing specific goals, and it provides a structure through which the sales professional can move ahead.

Business sales plans vary, but most include these major sections: introduction and executive summary, in-depth description of sales territory and industry, market analysis and trends, and sales projections.

Further, peak sales performers develop a marketing plan that includes: focused tactics to identify prospects; reach and intrigue them with messages that cut through competitive clutter; and educate them about the product or service.

Essentially, peak sales performers are the CEO's of their own destiny. They operate their desk as an independent business, focused on profit and productivity. They know their customers, the issues they face, and the role each client plays in the overall purchase process. For this reason, you'll often find peak sales performers talking directly with those who make actual buying decisions while avoiding time expenditures on those who have no real power.

■ *Magnum P.I. Selling*

In finding these decision-makers, sales professionals sometimes act as detectives, searching out clues needed to locate and pinpoint the most important contact in a company. (Return to this book's opening chapters to review the many resources that are useful in this sleuthing process.)

Peak sales performers not only understand their customers and the general business climate, they understand the sales process, which includes these steps:

■ Prospect

■ Qualify

■ Provide Interest

■ Gain Conviction

■ Conduct Demonstrations

■ Handle Objections

■ Close

Recognizing where you are in the sales process is important to gauging your progress and staying on track. Peak sales performers can accurately identify their point in this process—an important ability that contributes to their success.

I mentioned earlier that sales is like a roller coaster. You must be prepared to ride the peaks and valleys of success and failure. Doing so requires you to be confident in your abilities, your product, and your company. The more confident you are, the better you become at delivering superb customer service.

By recognizing some of the key traits of peak sales performers, you can emulate them and begin reaping rewards. Start by renewing your commitment to the sales profession, setting goals, thinking of new ways to deliver better customer service, planning your next sales call, and understanding your customers. Don't procrastinate—act like a true peak performer and start now!

"No sale is really complete until the product is worn out, and the customer is satisfied."

—L.L. Bean, American Businessman, Founder of L.L. Bean

SELLING SCORECARD

List three ideas from this chapter that you will put into immediate use to begin obtaining the results you seek.

☐ **Idea:**

_____

_____

_____

Start Date: _____

Finish Line Date: _____

☐ **Idea:**

_____

_____

_____

Start Date: _____

Finish Line Date: _____

☐ **Idea:**

_____

_____

_____

Start Date: _____

Finish Line Date: _____

EVENT:

PERFORMERS

chapter 14

Secrets of Winning Salespeople

E ven before the tragedy of Sept. 11, 2001, the U.S. economy was beginning to take a nose dive. Since then, customers have revisited everything from budgets, to personnel, to company parties, and benefits. While this may seem like new economic territory, sales professionals should remain unflustered by these changes.

I've already mentioned the 80/20 Rule in a couple of different contexts earlier in this book. In this instance, it is evident that 20 percent of sales professionals get 80 percent of the business. And when I survey salespeople, they are concerned that they may not be in that golden 20 percent. They want more, and they are perplexed about what separates merely adequate sales professionals from high achievers.

We all strive to be the best. Sales managers clearly want the best and CEO's clamor for the best sales staff they can employ. So what, then, is the correct formula for bringing in more business? The answer lies in the secrets of highly effective sales professionals:

■ Customer Knowledge

One of the pet peeves that sales managers have regarding their sales staff is a salesperson who lacks a clear understanding of the client. In today's very fast and competitive world, a sales professional cannot afford to lack this crucial understanding.

During an annual performance review of a group of sales professionals, the sales manager asked each salesperson for specific account information. One of the salespeople became flustered when these questions were posed. Other than noting that the client was a multinational pharmaceutical company, the salesperson knew little else. It is no wonder that this individual was not as successful as he could have been.

Customers expect you to understand their business. They are looking for solutions to an array of important business issues, and they expect you to have the appropriate answers. If you do not understand your client's issues from a business and industry perspective, you simply cannot provide the solutions that the client seeks, and you are less likely to make the sale.

The steps to understanding your client have been reiterated several times in this book. Do your homework, and you'll be rewarded.

■ Questioning Aptitude

You'll surely recognize this familiar scenario: You get home from a long day of work, sit down to a hot meal, begin to unwind – and the telephone rings. You reluctantly pick up the phone, only to hear a salesperson hawking a product or service. The salesperson reads from a script and does not ask a single question. There's no incentive to listen to this uninvited sales pitch. You hang up.

The best sales professionals engage their audience. Therefore, the first task of the sales professional during any type of encounter with a potential buyer, must be to question the customer. Questions allow you to gain useful information, such as consumer behavior, decision criteria, budgets, time frame, and competition. Since clients typically do not offer this information, it is important for the salesperson to ask for it by using open-ended questions.

Instead of asking, "Do you have a budget for this project," ask the customer, "If you had a budget for this product what might it look like and when might you decide to make a purchase?" The revision leads the client to think through the possibility of using your product and requesting purchase money. In addition, clients who respond to open-ended questions provide more information and set the stage for more qualifying questions and potential sales objections.

Finally, asking the right questions allows the salesperson to learn more about the next habit described below.

■ Accurate Interpretation of Consumers' Wants and Needs

There are several paths that a salesperson can follow during a sales presentation; however, the most important one leads to a complete understanding of the buyer's wants and needs.

In order to sell anything to anyone, an effective sales professional must question the customer to discover why they want or need the product. Many sales managers report that, despite plenty of exuberance, their sales force is not effective in closing sales. Through analysis, we discover that these ineffective salespeople are excited, but they are so busy talking about product that they fail to ask questions. This communication breakdown takes the focus off the customer and his or her wants and needs. Without uncovering need, what can you possibly sell?

The familiar solution here, which connects directly to the habit above, is to ask so many open-ended questions that your presentations become conversational. This will take some practice, but once you master the art of solid questioning, you can formulate questions that hone in on wants and needs. When you do this, your sales increase.

One final point about wants and needs: customers will purchase from you for personal and/or professional reasons. Remember to ask yourself, "What's in it for the customer?" Is he or she looking for job recognition, cost effectiveness, or personal happiness with your product? As you progress with your line of questioning, try to uncover the "truth of purchase."

■ Ability to Establish Client Rapport

Without question, building a relationship with your customer is vital. Good relationships with clients enable you to create long-term sales success, which is why client relationships are like long-term investments.

■ Uncanny Ability to Ride the Sales Roller Coaster

Sales is a volatile process. One day is favorable, the next sullen, the next euphoric, and so on. Each day brings a new experience, challenge, and adventure. In order to be an effective sales professional, you must be flexible and adapt well to change. Each opportunity, sales call, and presentation opens new doors and offers new insights.

I often tell my clients to become a chameleon and adjust to the changing landscape. If you do not, you will become frustrated, and your customers will sense that there is a problem. Think of customers as mirrors: they mimic your behavior. If you are happy, your customers are happy; if you are angry, frustrated, or scared, they are too.

Since my first days as a sales professional, I have carried a small pocket mirror to every sales appointment. I look at the mirror prior to my call and assure myself that I appear to be happy or neutral. I notice my facial expressions and body posture. By projecting a positive attitude and a neutral posture, I enable customers to feel at ease, oblivious to my trials and tribulations. I focus on the customer's want and needs and his or her contentment with my product and personal service.

■ Understands the "Knows" Principle

I love sales professionals who are know-it-alls. At least, I love sales professionals who understand the "knows" of the sales business.

As you know by now, it is important to thoroughly know your customer or prospect, product or service, topic you are going to speak about when you meet with the customer, competitors, marketplace, questions you plan to ask, possible objections, closing technique, limitations, and factors that determine what you can and cannot commit to.

■ Honesty and Enthusiasm

In sales, as in many professions, success comes much easier to those who love what they do, love their product, and love the people they work with. But sales are especially reliant upon professionals who can honestly express enthusiasm for their work. Dishonesty or lack of enthusiasm can be the death knell of a sales call.

By bringing these habits along every time you go to work, your chances of success will increase exponentially, and you are likely to be more satisfied with your work and, hence, your life.

> *I don't measure a man's success by how high he climbs,*
> *but how high he bounces when he hits bottom.*
> —General George S. Patton

SELLING SCORECARD

List three ideas from this chapter that you will put into immediate use to begin obtaining the results you seek.

☐ **Idea:**

_____

_____

_____

Start Date: _____

Finish Line Date: _____

☐ **Idea:**

_____

_____

_____

Start Date: _____

Finish Line Date: _____

☐ **Idea:**

_____

_____

_____

Start Date: _____

Finish Line Date: _____

EVENT:

SECRETS

chapter 15

10 Greatest Sales Mistakes & How to Overcome Them

A s a sales manager, I worked hard to help my staff recognize and overcome common mistakes. Even after I became a speaker and consultant, I noticed that questions about the same errors would come up in various sales seminars and training sessions.

By understanding these mistakes and their resolutions, you can learn from others and avoid these pitfalls.

■ Lack of Preparation

Sales professionals must be prepared for sales calls and presentations. The chapter on presentation skills outlined a variety of strategies for ensuring adequate preparation. Simply put, more thorough preparation leads to more sales success.

Again, I cannot overstate the importance of research and detailed planning. Carry notes and supporting facts with you on sales calls in case you need to cite quick statistics or sources. And remember that employees move frequently. Your previous contact may no longer be in the same position. Always check before you call to ensure that you have current contact information.

Arm yourself with the information you need to feel confident of your ability to speak knowledgeably and answer questions or objections in an intelligent manner.

▪ *Lack of Good Communication/Listening*

Sales professionals tend to be great orators. We love to talk. But, as I've stated several times already, knowing when to stop talking is just as important as knowing what to say. More than one salesperson has talked himself out of a sale when he should have simply been quiet and walked away with a signed contract.

The previous chapter noted that a questioning aptitude is one of the traits of a highly successful sales professional. Yet asking the right questions is only half of the equation. Listening to the client's answers is equally important. Take notes while listening and consider the issues raised. Use this information to help you determine exactly how your product or service will address the client's needs.

When speaking with a client, never interrupt. It is simply rude and conveys the feeling that you do not care about the client. Interruption will not create rapport. To become a better listener:

Pause—When speaking with a client, don't be afraid to pause. In fact, silently counting to seven before plunging ahead with more chatter will allow the client to add more information to a previous statement and give you an opportunity to digest the information in order to ask better follow-up questions.

You can practice this powerful technique while talking with family and friends. People may seem uncomfortable during the pause, but the ability to be silent while awaiting more information is crucial to sales negotiations.

Ask—This book has mentioned the importance of asking appropriate questions many times and has reviewed several techniques for effectively questioning clients. Closed-ended and open-ended questions are useful, as is the ability to answer a question with another question. (Several examples of this appear earlier in the text.)

Paraphrase—Rephrasing what you have heard the client say and repeating it back to him or her is a valuable technique for ensuring that you understand the client's point. It also proves to the client that you have been paying attention, which will help build rapport and trust.

Summarize—Similar to paraphrasing, summarizing allows you to consolidate the information for better comprehension. Summaries also provide natural transitions as you move to new topics and enable you to close the conversation when needed.

■ Sending Unnecessary Literature

Nothing can annoy a prospective buyer more than unwanted email or snail mail. Consumers are busy and may say, "Can you just send me the information?" in order to end an unsolicited sales call. In this case, you may send the requested information, but never pelt a customer with written material unless you have made personal contact first.

Consider this: hundreds of thousands of dollars in marketing materials are thrown away, in many cases without even being looked at by the recipient.

Instead of becoming a source of annoyance, take the time to qualify your sales leads and make personal contact. If a customer gives you the "send me information" line, ask what specific information he or she seeks so that you can tailor a package especially for that individual. This step, which shows that you care about the customer's needs and wants, will set you apart from most salespeople. Your ability to be personal, honest, and respectful certainly will result in more sales.

Stop sending information and start sending conversation to your clients!

■ Lack of Interest from You

The buyer can sense your interest level through verbal and nonverbal cues. Your appearance and demeanor are important in communicating your degree of interest. If you dress well and appear pleasant and attentive, the client will know that you have a real interest in working with them to solve problems.

Your voice and body language are also powerful tools in conveying interest and enthusiasm. Speak with passion and conviction. Look alert and exhibit good posture. Passion drives the sales process and is vital to closing the sale. It paves your path to success.

▪ *Failing to Review Sales Appointments*

Just as professional athletes review tapes of their games or events, sales-people should review their sales call performance.

Sales is unique in its level of competition and volatility. Honest self-evaluation will help give you an edge over other salespeople who want to make the same sale that you do.

▪ *Misunderstanding the "Gatekeeper"*

The decision-maker in an organization is often "guarded" by a gate-keeper. So it behooves you to build a professional relationship with that person.

By understanding when you fit within the organizational construct, you become an asset to the company. If you can provide a benefit to the gatekeeper, you also will become more valuable to the decision-maker. For instance, you might say, "The reason I am calling is because I work with organizations like yours that…" By demonstrating that you un-derstand the company mission and vision, you align yourself with the organization.

Most salespeople view gatekeepers as merely an obstacle to reaching their intended target. To an extent, this is an accurate characterization. Gatekeepers receive numerous calls from salespeople, so you must dif-ferentiate yourself from others.

▪ *Inefficient Planning or Fact Finding*

It is imperative that you plan every sales call. Failure to plan will result in the client viewing you as nothing more than an unwelcome interrup-tion. The worst thing you can do is waste a client's time.

To avoid this, return to our familiar tactics of research and appropriate questioning techniques. You may even want to prioritize and script your questions before the call. Always include more questions than you actu-ally intend to ask so that you are prepared for any twist and turn in the conversation.

■ *Misunderstanding Objections*

A previous chapter dealt in detail with client objections and methods for overcoming them. Plan to address the client's objections, and you will be far ahead in the sales race.

If you view them as learning opportunities for the client and a chance for you to better understand his or her issues and concerns, you can begin to enjoy dealing with objections.

■ *Failing to Gain Commitment*

We reviewed a variety of closing techniques earlier in this book. Don't forget to ask for the sale and use an appropriate close.

■ *Action Plan Summary*

These are just a few of the most common mistakes made in sales. It takes at least 21 days to change a behavior. (See the 21 Day Action Planner on page 88.) Be patient with yourself as you practice overcoming these sales errors. With time and persistence, you'll gain mastery over your technique, blot out the negative behaviors, and replace them with constructive activities.

"For every sale you miss because you're too enthusiastic, you will miss a hundred because you're not enthusiastic enough."

—Zig Ziglar

SELLING SCORECARD

List three ideas from this chapter that you will put into immediate use to begin obtaining the results you seek.

☐ **Idea:**

_____

_____

_____

Start Date: _____

Finish Line Date: _____

☐ **Idea:**

_____

_____

_____

Start Date: _____

Finish Line Date: _____

☐ **Idea:**

_____

_____

_____

Start Date: _____

Finish Line Date: _____

EVENT:

MISTAKES

chapter 16

Account Management— Large & Small

Diversification and specialization were hot topics a couple of decades ago. For example, if your hurt your arm, you visited an orthopedist instead of a general practitioner. The sales profession also became more specialized as accounts grew more complex.

Account management is no different today than it was when this trend began. Account managers must understand the complexities of the account. They are responsible for learning about the client's business, seeking new opportunities for growth, and anticipating the client's future needs. In some ways, account managers serve as relationship specialists.

Sales quotas may exist, but sales growth is strategic, not tactical. Account managers think in terms of future trends and anticipate the changing corporate landscape.

■ *B2B or R4R*

Today's technical society includes many confusing terms and acronyms. For instance, B2B is shorthand for "business to business."

While many organizations use electronic data interchange and other technical means to engage each other and maintain production, this is not possible in sales. Many people still fear the Internet and believe that electronic commerce hurts a company's ability to serve and support clients. This is simply untrue.

Customers crave relationships. Admittedly, for numerous items Internet sales are quick and easy, yet most buyers want a relationship with a sales representative who will become a long-term partner in proactive problem resolution. Enter the account manager.

Because account managers specialize in relationships, they don't worry about B2B. Instead, they focus on R4R, the "Relationship for the Betterment of the Relationship."

Today's account manager is like a consultant, serving as a concerned advocate on behalf of the client. They acquire knowledge about the client's organization and assist in resolving issues, gaining efficiency, and reducing overhead. Good account managers build that all-important rapport and are excellent listeners.

One might even consider an account manager similar to a project manager. These individuals oversee many aspects of the account, such as vertical sales, client support, and technical and accounting issues. In some cases, account managers are responsible for multiple locations and accounts.

One of the main keys to account management involves the ability to fully understand all account issues. Therefore, account managers must be prepared to address these issues at all times. An account management planning guide is a critical tool that provides information about account history, contacts, issues, and revenue. The plan covers several critical areas, which are identified below:

■ Account Profile

One of the first steps in creating an account management plan is to build an account profile, which includes the company name, industry background, and the company's current gross revenue. Also included are the names of the executive and senior staff, the lines of business, and pertinent contact information. Most of this data can be found in company information databases.

Other pertinent data includes: a listing of the board of directors, competitors, number of employees, and current sales figures for the account. This information should fit on a single sheet of paper, providing a snapshot of the account that can be used for management reporting.

The second page of the account management profile should include
a section on current products, account issues, installation locations,
and contact information for all sales representatives that service the account.

Account Profile

Account Name: _____

Address1: _____

Address2: _____

City: _____ State: __ Country: _____ Postal Code: _____

Telephone: _____

Facsimile: _____

URL: _____

Gross Revenue: _____

CEO: _____

CFO: _____

COO: _____

Lines of Business: _____

Number of Employees: _____

Board of Directors: _____
_____

Competitors: _____
_____

Products: _____
_____

Current Spent with the Account:
_____

_____

■ Who/What/Won't

Next, list the names of important contacts within the client organization as well as names of individuals that you should avoid. Note both current and future contacts, including decision-makers. It is important to also include influencers and recommenders.

Identify people within the company whom you want to meet and include their title, potential purchase, areas of influence, and what you can help them with.

Selling is like sport. One must have a good offense and a good defense. Part of your defense is understanding the coaches, players, and opponents. Therefore, list individuals who may hinder your account management abilities. Those who are partial to current vendors or have a negative history with sales teams should appear on this list.

Decision-Maker: _____

Champion: _____

Influencer(s): _____

Recommender(s): _____

Coach: _____

Those Against Me: _____

■ Client Review

The client review should include current information about the client, industry reports, and competitive market action. If the client is a publicly held company, all this information will be readily available. It is also available for private firms, although it may be somewhat harder to obtain. One of the best tools at your disposal is the Internet. (See the list of online resources listed earlier in the book.)

Now list your competitors who also have a stake in the account. Document what the competitor provides to the client and why that competitor has a relationship with your client's company. If possible, include information on the competitor's account representative and that individual's contact within the client company. Complete the competitive profile with a SWOTT analysis.

■ SWOTT Analysis

In fact, it is important to prepare a SWOTT analysis on your own services, too. What are the market conditions necessary for increasing your installation base? What areas are vulnerable? Where are future growth opportunities? What threatens to compromise the account? How are service-level agreements perceived? Who are your account's champions and opponents? Do not skimp on the answers. Be resourceful, thorough, and complete.

As detailed on pages 111 to 112, SWOTT is an abbreviation for Strengths, Weaknesses, Opportunities, Threats and Trends.

As an account manager, include a SWOTT analysis in your management planning guide to help you maintain accounts and profitability. Even if you are early in your sales career, and account management seems like a distant professional destination, the principles of creating such detailed account management documentation can be helpful in allowing you to progress up the sales ladder.

■ Client Opportunity/Forecast

Next, outline opportunities for advancement. Define the client's wants and the needs as they relate to future trends. Detail your goals for the next 6, 12, and 18 months. Identify all areas that offer growth potential. Explain why the client will want the benefits provided by your product or service. Finally, list all sales-related activities that will require personnel support.

Follow this forecast with a complete financial analysis. It is advisable to use a table or spreadsheet to categorize your goals and anticipated sales growth by location and month.

No account management plan is complete without 30-, 60-, and 90-day action plans. Consider the resources needed and the measurement techniques that will help you document your progress. Specify clearly what support or resources you will need from various departments within your company. Account managers do not fly solo. It takes cooperation, collaboration, and commitment to successfully manage an account.

■ Successful Account Management

Sales professionals typically act alone. Account managers do not. Successful account management is a collaborative process. Because today's business environment is multifaceted, complex, and diversified, attention to detail and time management skills are important factors to successful account maintenance.

Companies want people they know and trust to assist in creating a successful business. The account manager is a key player.

Follow the steps outlined in this chapter to obtain Finish Line results and provide Gold Medal customer service!

There are no traffic jams along the extra mile.

—Roger Staubach

SELLING SCORECARD

List three ideas from this chapter that you will put into immediate use to begin obtaining the results you seek.

☐ *Idea:*

_____

_____

_____

Start Date: _____

Finish Line Date: _____

☐ *Idea:*

_____

_____

_____

Start Date: _____

Finish Line Date: _____

☐ *Idea:*

_____

_____

_____

Start Date: _____

Finish Line Date: _____

EVENT:

ACCOUNT MANAGEMENT

PART 3:

Coaching Clinic

chapter 17

Developing a Killer Sales Force

One of the most fundamental challenges that sales managers face is the development of a powerful sales team. Finding good help isn't always easy, but there are a few principles that can assist you in making the best possible decisions:

■ Hiring the Right Fit

Managers should be *ABLE: Always Be Looking for Employees.* Keep your eyes open for potential hires in all your professional interactions, even within your own company. Seek people who are extroverted, easy to speak with, and bursting with energy.

Good prospective hires also have a hunger for success. Salespeople crave interaction with others, monetary compensation, and challenges. Look for candidates who exhibit this voracious appetite for success and talk about their goals and commitment. Ask questions that challenge their thinking and listen for comments that indicate the candidate's ideas are aligned with your corporate goals and sales quotas. A good sales candidate will treat a job interview like a sales presentation.

I once interviewed a candidate for a telemarketing position. She brought several important items with her to the interview: a fresh copy of her resume; detailed information about the company's products, which showed that she had taken the time to research the company prior to our conversation; and information about competitors' products and how they differed from the product she would be selling.

I was so impressed with her preparation, tenacity, and enthusiasm, I hired her on the spot! She proved to be my best sales representative and served as a model for others.

One novel, but surprisingly effective, hiring approach involves allowing your staff to conduct job interviews. In assessing potential coworkers, they will naturally gravitate to candidates who are a good fit with the existing sales team. Your staff also can provide valuable feedback on new hires.

Don't neglect to ask job candidates about the movies they watch, books they read, and tapes they listen to. Are they interested in nonfiction books and tapes that bolster their sales skills? Are they willing to consider sales a nonstop profession?

It takes time to find talent, and you may make mistakes along the way. However, by following these tips, you will build a solid and productive sales team.

■ *The Hot and the Not!*

New demands, new challenges, and ever-present changes have made our work more intense and stressful. Most people feel short on time, short on job security, and long on financial and professional risks.

Changes in technology have fostered changes in the workplace. There is a high demand for skilled and knowledgeable workers.

Companies are constantly working to meet today's changing professional demands. Job loyalty and security seem like things of the past. People want freedom, creative opportunities, and job satisfaction in addition to a paycheck.

Global business, politics, and culture invite more diversity of values, lifestyles, and tastes. Sales managers must work with many different types of people while inspiring performance, speed, creativity, and initiative. They must empower employees to make independent decisions followed by appropriate action.

Some of their other pressing challenges facing today's sales managers are listed below.

■ Doesn't Know What's Expected

Goals are vital to individual and organizational success. Managers should work with staff to define territories, roles, and responsibilities.

While time is at a premium, meetings need not be lengthy. Fifteen minutes once or twice per month can enable proper communication. Investing 15 minutes today will prevent aggravation and missed sales quotas tomorrow. The best managers communicate and teach their staff, encouraging mutual trust, and honesty.

■ Isn't Aware of a Problem

Sales professionals quickly recognize problems with territories or accounts. Solving these problems often requires consultation with the sales manager. Taking time to nip problems in the bud is crucial to avoiding more serious issues down the road.

All employees require direction, and sales professionals who work independently may feel out of touch with the company and a larger sales force. Don't let a lack of communication create a void in the manager-employee relationship. Managers are like coaches, constantly instructing and providing feedback.

■ Lack of Encouragement

Sales professionals require regular encouragement. It is incumbent upon the manager to motivate the sales team. Although I stated earlier that sales is a profession requiring a degree of self-motivation, a simple pat on the back from the sales manager is a powerful motivator. In addition, performance reviews should be conducted annually and can provide another source of encouragement.

Face-to-face communication is the best way to instill motivation, although email has become increasingly popular. Give your sales team regular opportunities to talk with one another and share tips and tactics.

■ *Punished for Taking a Risk*

Selling requires risk. Therefore, mistakes should not be penalized. However, managers can guide their sales teams in taking appropriate risks by mentoring them through the sales planning process. Punishment leads to fear, which can hinder the salesperson in future client interactions and create a negative work atmosphere.

■ *Not Interested or Motivated*

Sales professionals are born and made. They are usually born extroverts. And with training they learn the necessary skills to approach a prospective client, negotiate, and close a sale. Managers should not be too anxious to hire "fully loaded" sales professionals who feel they have no more need for professional development.

Instead, I recommend that managers interview and hire salespeople with 60 to 75 percent of the complete skill set. These candidates typically welcome challenges and are eager to learn in order to become top-level performers. Such motivation is a boon to the sales team.

Keeping sales professionals challenged and motivated can be an ongoing management issue. However, managers and sales staff have many opportunities for mutual instruction. Maintaining high energy and nurturing a learning environment helps motivate the sales team, which is a key to decreasing attrition.

■ *Managing by Fear*

There are thousands of books about leadership, and they all seem to discuss the charisma, charm, vision, and values of today's leaders. They do not advise readers on how to create fear and hostility.

No sales professional wants to work for a dictator. Do not manage through fear. Doing so will create distrust, dislike, and discord. When fear is removed from the work environment, employee morale and productivity will soar.

■ *Feedback*

Throughout this chapter, the importance of communication has been emphasized. Feedback is another important form of manager-employee communication and can be provided during regular sales team meetings and performance reviews.

Communicate with your sales team during both challenging and celebratory times. Praise them when they meet a quota or gain a new client. Let them know that you care about their performance and coach them to success.

■ Training & Development

Workplace learning is the smartest strategic solution to the biggest human resource problem ever to face employers. Well-trained people perform better and stay longer. It's such a simple win-win solution. Invest more in employee growth and reap great benefits in high performance, improved efficiency, and longer tenure. It can be done. It must be done. Workers want more training.

The more training workers receive, the more likely they are to be satisfied with their employers. Conversely, workers not offered training are significantly less likely to be satisfied and more inclined to look for a new employer.

The average U.S. company loses half of its employees every four years. Development Dimension International of Bridgeville, Penn., surveyed 150 Fortune 500 companies to learn that the average company expects 33 percent turnover at the executive level in the next five years and a full one-third said they're not confident that they will be able to find suitable replacements.

In addition, "an article in Business Week reports that among employees who say their company offers poor training, 41 percent plan to leave within a year versus 12 percent of those who rate opportunities as excellent. The survey pegs the cost of losing a typical worker at $50,000. So a 1,000-worker company with poor training could lose $20.5 million, while non-existent mentoring could cost $9 million." (ASTD)

Many sales professionals do not want training because they believe it takes times away from the pursuit of sales. However, nothing is more important than a quick review of fundamental selling or communication skills. Training increases accountability. When accountability increases so, too, does productivity. In order to gain the productivity you require, training might only be necessary two to four times per year.

■ *Reward and Recognition*

This is one of the most sensitive areas in today's business climate, especially as it relates to sales professionals. Unlike most groups, sales professionals tend to work independently, and one might assume that this maverick spirit results in a decreased need for third-party recognition. While awards for meeting quotas and achieving special accomplishments are common, many organizations do not conduct awards ceremonies or adequately recognize positive efforts.

Sales professionals ride a daily emotional roller coaster. They fight for revenue and try to enhance their organization's operational base. In fact, sales is the bedrock of business success. Because sales professionals are compensated well for achieving success, many businesspeople feel that additional rewards are unnecessary. However, like all employees, sales professionals should be recognized by management.

A recent *Salary.com* survey (November 2005) found that 65 percent of employees look for new jobs because they become frustrated, discouraged, and bored. This is a harmful business trend. Employers can retain workers and increase productivity by offering opportunities for growth. The workforce is a company's most important asset, so recognition is crucial.

Some surveys indicate that employees leave because they are not paid enough. For sales professionals this is not true. Salespeople want to be challenged and, like others, want to be recognized for their achievements in the field. It is easy to search for employment in a new organization but similar issues will crop up.

So what is a manager to do? Simply recognize an outstanding staff. Coaches recognize and encourage outstanding players. Religious leaders praise their deity.

There are several low-cost techniques that can provide employee recognition. Thank-you cards, post-it notes, letters of commendation, and certificates are inexpensive and show appreciation for a job well done.

If you are able to invest a bit more; gift cards, movie passes, theater tickets, car washes, and dinner reservations are popular perks. Read *1,001 Ways to Reward Employees,* by Bob Nelson for more creative ideas.

You want to reward your staff on a consistent basis but keep the recognition fresh, well-deserved, and unexpected.

The tools presented in this chapter will give you a starting point for your management career. Sales management is challenging, but with the proper techniques you can build a wildly successful sales team.

> *Teams do not go physically flat,*
> *they go mentally stale.*
>
> —Vincent Lombardi

SELLING SCORECARD

List three ideas from this chapter that you will put into immediate use to begin obtaining the results you seek.

☐ **Idea:**

_____

_____

_____

Start Date: _____

Finish Line Date: _____

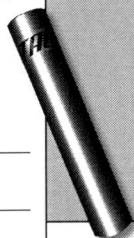

☐ **Idea:**

_____

_____

_____

Start Date: _____

Finish Line Date: _____

☐ **Idea:**

_____

_____

_____

Start Date: _____

Finish Line Date: _____

EVENT:

DEVELOPING A KILLER SALES FORCE

chapter 18

Sales Management & Sales Leadership

One of the most challenging aspects of selling is managing sales-people. It is difficult to monitor the activities and profitability of the corporate entrepreneur. Sales professionals want to be free of administrative and operational issues. They don't like supervision.

One of the underlying issues that I see in organizations today is that sales professionals report to former peers. It is very difficult to take someone from the field and have former colleagues report to that individual. More importantly, sales professionals who are promoted to management often are given no management training.

A sales manager can be a leader, but good leaders do not necessarily make good managers and vice versa. Do not confuse management with leadership. Successful leaders choose good sales managers in order to delegate tasks and responsibilities.

■ Managers

Managers are people who do things right, and leaders are people who do the right thing. Thus, sales managers concern themselves with the procurement, coordination, and distribution of resources needed by the sales team. The manager also facilitates an organization's work by en-suring that activities follow the organization's rules and regulations.

A manager is similar to a football quarterback. He is the key player when executing a play. He ensures that the other players are aligned correctly on the field and run the designed patterns. Sales managers ensure that the salespeople understand their role and complete their assigned tasks.

The corporate leader, like a head coach, designs the plays and creates a team environment by preparing and planning.

Management is defined as: 1) the act or art of managing: the conducting or supervising of something (as a business); 2) judicious use of means to accomplish an end; and 3) the collective body of those who manage or direct an enterprise. A manager ensures success of policies, procedures, and practices. He or she is not only concerned with feelings or team spirit. The manager's main concern is with specific project completion.

■ Leaders

In contrast to management, leadership is a complex process through which a person influences others to accomplish a mission, task, or objective and directs the organization in a way that makes it more cohesive and coherent. Leaders carry out this process by applying their leadership attributes: beliefs, values, ethics, character, knowledge, and skills.

Although managers have authority to accomplish certain tasks and objectives, this power does not make them leaders. Leaders inspire people to achieve goals and motivate them to continued success. Different skills are needed for different leadership roles.

There are two primary purposes of leadership: to inspire innovation and creativity and to motivate participation and achievement. A successful mid-level corporate leader can inspire and motivate employees, staff members, and managers. Inspiration and motivation are dynamic terms, and the energy, aura, and environment produced by strong leadership affect everyone who comes in contact with that leader.

A unified mission, shared aspirations, and universal goals and values are essential for strong, successful leadership to flourish. Leaders can enter an environment of disorder, discord, drift, fear, aimlessness, confusion, mistrust, or paranoia, and unite employees as a team that has purpose, direction, objectives, and a positive attitude.

A truly successful leader is a "people person" who has "been there and done that"—a person coworkers can identify with. The leader creates a sense in each coworker that everyone can make a difference, and, at the end of each day, each coworker feels that he or she *has* made a difference.

■ Success and Motivation

To be a successful sales leader one must know how to choose good managers who are effective in completing delegated responsibilities. Failure to recognize this dependence on managers has caused some of the business's most brilliant leaders to briefly excite their industry, only to fizzle like a burned-out firecracker. They have no foundation for lasting success.

Managers must be detail-oriented to be successful; leaders must be concept-oriented and able to see the big picture. Good leaders usually dislike details; good managers may have a hard time seeing beyond them. Of course there are exceptions. A handful of effective managers are blessed with leadership ability, and some leaders are also good managers. However, the most effective leadership comes from a partnership of those who lead and those who manage - a partnership that allows each to concentrate on his or her own role.

A manager looks at what is; a leader looks at what is possible. It takes both qualities—one without the other is ultimately doomed to mediocrity or failure. If managers understood leadership and leaders understood management, both would be more effective.

"The leader's job is to give the managers direction, vision, and inspiration. Regardless of how good the leader is, he will be ineffective without good managers. His degree of success or failure will be determined by the quality of managers he can recruit. Discerning the quality and ability of his people and using them properly is just as important in accomplishing goals as having the vision and other resources required for the enterprise."

In addition to flexibility and vision, leaders must have the ability to develop and articulate a value proposition, maintain it in a dynamic market, and encourage others to buy into it. They also must create a culture that values mentorship and learning. It will be the learning organization that makes change easier and assists in creative production and harmony. The would-be leaders who are unwilling or unable to demonstrate these behaviors will find themselves with few followers.

■ *Turn Employees Into Owners*

By enabling each employee to become CEO of his or her professional life, some companies provide an environment where ideas can be shared, people can learn, and employees matter. The way to get more productive employees and create a competitive spirit is to unleash the power of the individual.

Jack Welch, former CEO of General Electric, felt that by turning employees loose to excel within the company, fresh ideas and innovation would flow on a daily basis. It is from this process that productivity and profitability increase. I believe this is true of the sales professional – make him the CEO of his territory and watch the sales soar!

■ *Should Sales Managers Teach for Peak Performance?*

Leaders go beyond the development of a common vision; they value the human resources of their organizations. They provide an environment that promotes individual contributions to the organization's work.

Leaders develop and maintain collaborative relationships formed during the development and adoption of that shared vision. They form teams, support team efforts, develop skills groups, and provide the necessary resources—both human and material—to fulfill the shared corporate vision.

One of today's best methods used to motivate a workforce is training and coaching. Though it might seem that the practice of business coaching began recently—and suddenly—the concept of assisting business professionals on an individual basis is not new.

In the past, business professionals who were deficient in a particular area, such as interpersonal skills, were referred to internal consultants, such as industrial psychologists.

Just like an athlete training to become the best in his or her sport, today's business professional is seeking better, faster, and more efficient ways to be recognized, respected, and be better at what they do. To that end, leaders seek coaches to make them more effective at their jobs, in personal relationships, and when encouraging employee productivity and efficiency.

■ *Training & Coaching*

It is important to note that training and coaching are two different things, although some people use the terms interchangeably. Training is a structured lesson designed to provide the employee with the knowledge and skills to perform a task. Coaching, on the other hand, is a process designed to help the employee gain greater competence and overcome barriers in order to improve job performance.

For instance, when you were in school, the gym teacher (trainer) taught you how to play basketball. You went out for the school team because you had a basic understanding of the game and its rules – but the coach taught you the finer points of the game. In business, a coach works with an individual to refine skills and assist in attaining excellence in the field.

As you can see, training and coaching go hand-in-hand. First you train employees with lots of technical support, and then you coach them with motivational pointers. And only a leader can be a motivator.

Training and coaching help create the conditions that cause someone to learn and develop. People learn by example; by forming a picture in their minds of what they are trying to learn; by gaining and understanding necessary information; by applying it to their job; and by practice.

The best sales managers/sales leaders help employees gain peak productivity through these activities:

- **Evaluate** to determine knowledge, skill, and confidence levels.

- **Define** objectives that can be measured periodically and break them down into step-by-step actions.

- **Clarify** direction, goals, and accountability. To foster accountability, involve the person or team in the decision-making.

- **Encourage** peer coaching by reminding employees that everyone has a stake in each other's success.

- **Coaching** is more than telling people how to do something. It involves giving advice, skill-building, creating challenges, removing performance barriers, building better processes, and learning through discovery.

- **Deal** with emotional obstacles by helping them through change, reviewing, pointing out ways that employees hold themselves back, comforting when they become confused, etc.

- **Give** feedback by pointing towards solutions and stay away from critiquing errors.

- **Lead** by example. Demonstrate the desired behaviors.

Leaders recognize that accolades stimulate motivation. They understand employees simply want to be noticed and understood. They do not want to be treated like a number or a liability; their efforts and responsibilities collectively assist in organizational growth. Although not as important to the manager, recognition appeals to the personality and growth of the individual.

Contrasting this belief is management. Since managers look at process, procedure, and policy as the foundation to organizational success, there is resistance to training. As depicted throughout this analysis, managers feel training is a drain on resources, time, and profit.

This practical approach reinforces the mechanistic nature of management and the inability to motivate employees. Individuals look for management to invest in their future, and, when training is required, it typically is created to address process and procedural flow—not to enhance employee motivation and teamwork.

Managers must recognize their mechanistic approaches and become more sympathetic to employee needs. They must recognize that employees are individuals with feelings, desires, needs, and goals. Employers need to understand that money is not the only thing that motivates people.

Today's employee wants to be happy on the job and content with his or her professional life. In order to be happier at work, employees want to reach the top of their hierarchy of needs, both personally and professionally. They want kudos for a job well done. Training and coaching are the catalysts that drive this happiness.

The new millennium signals a new beginning for society and business, and it brings a transformation of management to leadership. This change creates a renewal of management practices and the birth of new leaders. Clearly, the new millennium is about change. Business must change to become powerful, profitable, and proficient. Business professionals know that to do this, they must change their practices from management to leadership.

Employees of the 21st century are looking for guidance and for someone with a vision who can take them into uncharted waters and competently navigate. Leaders must have vision, faith, and the ability to ask and answer difficult questions. Key answers come through trial and error as well as experiential education. Certainly, without learning and knowledge, leaders fail. But with the proper guidance and education, future leaders are born.

Management practices and managers are vital to organizational function. Yet during the 1970's, 80's, and 90's, management did not create a unified and powerful workforce. Management practices from these decades create a figurative and literal "division of labor." Effective leadership removes these boundaries and creates cross-functioning teams and cohesive work environments.

Research indicates that there is a clear distinction between managers and leaders. While a manager can develop into a leader, I believe that much effort stems from employees in need of direction, mentoring, and motivation. Managers are typically apathetic to these needs, and their apathy shows in unimpressive corporate productivity.

Leading organizations build teams, create spirit, and bring cohesion where division previously existed. Leadership and teams functioned well for many Japanese companies during the 1980's. Now, they function well for companies like General Electric, Disney, and Microsoft.

Good management and good leadership are the combination for success. The proof is in the profit!

> *"Success seems to be connected with action.*
> *Successful people keep moving.*
> *They make mistakes, but they don't quit."*
>
> —Conrad Hilton

SELLING SCORECARD

List three ideas from this chapter that you will put into immediate use to begin obtaining the results you seek.

☐ **Idea:**

_____

_____

_____

Start Date: _____

Finish Line Date: _____

☐ **Idea:**

_____

_____

_____

Start Date: _____

Finish Line Date: _____

☐ **Idea:**

_____

_____

_____

Start Date: _____

Finish Line Date: _____

EVENT:

SALES MANAGEMENT & SALES LEADERSHIP

PART 4:

Go for Gold

chapter 19

Getting to the Finish Line

I n the era of global competition, home-based businesses, and "big, hairy, audacious goals," staying motivated in sales is difficult. Sales professionals are entrepreneurs at heart and riding the sales roller coaster is difficult at times. This is especially true when you are operating solo from a remote location or if you are always on the road.

Earlier in this book, I mentioned that sales are like riding a roller coaster. One day you are up, and the next day you could be down. Market economics, consumer demand, competition, and a plethora of personal and professional issues affect your sales efforts. So what is a sales professional to do?

■ *Read Motivational Books*

When you feel down and are looking for ways to climb back from the abyss, grab a motivational book off the shelf. Two of my favorites are *How to Win Friends and Influence People*, by Dale Carnegie and *The Greatest Salesman in the World*, by Og Mandino. These books are the bibles of the sales industry. Both were written more than 60 years ago, yet they still validate the many activities that sales professionals must undertake each day in order to stay motivated and cross the Finish Line of success. The Bible and books by Anthony Robbins also are favorites of mine when extra motivation is needed.

The only person who is preventing you from achieving success is you. In order to feel like a winner you must begin to change today. You have to believe that you can accomplish anything you set your mind on.

Several years ago I heard a song by Brian McKnight, entitled "Win," from the movie *Men of Honor*. The words explain how you can control your life and cope with daily issues so that you maintain a winning edge:

Never lose hope,

Never lose faith,

There's much too much at stake.

Upon myself I must depend,

I'm not looking for place or show,

Cause I'm gonna win!

When you get lost in your journey, these lyrics can place you back on the path of success and help you realize that you have already won!

■ Take a Break

For most sales professionals, selling is a 365-day-a-year, 7-days-a-week, 24-hours-a-day profession. We are always thinking about the next opportunity. We speak of our products at parties and family events, and we always read about new ways to sell services to new and existing customers. We continually hone our craft. However, much like the athlete that requires days off to recuperate from competition and practice, sales professionals need an occasional rest. Athletes get hurt when they are run down, employees become ill when too fatigued, and sales professionals lose sales when they become exhausted.

If you find yourself getting into a rut and you lack the motivation to continue, it's time to take a break. Go to a park, take a walk, watch a ball game, or read a book; do whatever you must to get away from the action until you feel more refreshed.

■ Look at Your Goals and Objectives

If you lack motivation, review your goals. Make sure that they follow the SMART formula that you read about earlier in this text. Consider new ways that you can achieve the success you long for and stay focused.

If your goals are not attainable, they may require in-depth assessment and review. Sit down with a friend or your sales manager and determine where adjustments might be required. If you use SMART goals, anything is possible, but you might need to alter your plans or adjust your time frame.

■ Participate in a Sales Contest

One of the best ways to stay motivated is to compete. No one likes to lose, but most sales professionals are born with a fierce competitive spirit and a need to succeed.

If you work for a small business with fewer than six sales professionals or if you are a sole proprietor with a home-based business, call your colleagues in sales or business and form a Finish Line Fan Club of 6 to 12 people.

The Finish Line Fan Club operates this way: First, arrange to call each other or meet in a central location on Monday. Each member of the circle contributes a mutually agreeable amount of cash ($5 or $10 is fine), which is given to the lucky winner. Your Finish Line Fan Club might decide to reward the member who makes the most telephone cold calls that week. Or perhaps the winner would be the individual who generates the most revenue during the week. There are many ways to determine who wins, depending on the member's goals and preferences.

By forming competitive and collegial peer groups, you can stay energized and keep each other on your toes. The result is that everyone can get to the Finish Line!

■ Are You on the Field or in the Stands?

Finish Line sales professionals are actively engaged in the sales game. They do not sit passively in the stands.

Selling is like a sport that requires salespeople to be athletically engaged in promoting and positioning your product with your target audience. In order to achieve sales success, you must actively pursue your markets and discover ways to attract positive attention so that consumers will buy your product or service.

■ Athletic Promotion

Public Speaking—It is to your benefit to speak to community and business organizations, chambers of commerce, peer groups, industry-specific groups and anyone else who will listen. Develop a presentation that incorporates the benefits of your product or service with the needs of the organization. This is one of the least expensive methods for marketing yourself and your product or service.

Consulting—Find opportunities to share the benefits of your skills integrated with your product offerings. Identify people who need your skill set and offer to assist them for a reasonable fee. Once they see the value that you provide, a "no" will be the furthest thing from their mind.

Writing Like public speaking, writing articles regarding your area of expertise is an inexpensive way to become a proactive and competitive sales athlete. Some sales professionals write up to 50 articles each month for various general and trade publications and newsletters. Publication can result in thousands, or even millions, of people becoming aware of your product or service. Your bottom line will improve as people read your articles, notice your byline, and later contact you. It's well worth sharing your thoughts and experience through the written word.

Networking—To actively promote your products and services, it pays to join as many professional and networking groups as time and money allow. Networking is the best way to get referrals, educate others about your product and share a platform for mutual success. Also useful are informal networks of peers with whom you share trials and tribulations, give and get advice, and learn new sales techniques.

■ Spectator Promotion

There are numerous things that you can do to promote your products and services without spending tremendous amounts of money and while remaining in the stands. Believe it or not, you can earn income without actively promoting your business. How? By doing things that make people remember your products and using methods that take little time and energy.

These things include:

Web Site—Your company's Web site informs both existing clients and prospects about your products and services. They can read about special promotions, sign up for electronic newsletters or periodic bulletins, and even order supplies and services. Can you imagine walking into your office first thing in the morning and finding 50 emails with orders for your product? You can actually sell your product when you are not actively selling!

If your business does not have a Web site, investigate getting one. There are some tricks to building a site that enable passive selling and there are many experts who can help you create your company's site. If you have the money, time, and energy to create this type of new distribution channel, an interactive web site is Finish Line selling at its best.

Customer Service—Your ability to create and maintain client rapport is key to your success. If you provide great service, clients will never forget you. Thank them for their business, offer advice, and consult them when needed and you will have a friend for life.

Great sales professionals know how to build relationships that will retain clients throughout their careers. If you want success, offer unparalleled service, support, and kindness.

Helpful Techniques—People want assistance with their problems. Another key to sales success is understanding client's needs and offering options to address their business issues. Take the time to understand your client's problems and offer as many helpful solutions as possible. This builds trust, empathy, and long-term business relationships.

"Desire is the key to motivation, but it's determination and commitment to an unrelenting pursuit of your goal —a commitment to excellence—that will enable you to attain the success you seek."

—Mario Andretti

SELLING SCORECARD

*List three ideas from this chapter that you will put into
immediate use to begin obtaining the results you seek.*

☐ **Idea:**

_____

_____

_____

Start Date: _____

Finish Line Date: _____

☐ **Idea:**

_____

_____

_____

Start Date: _____

Finish Line Date: _____

☐ **Idea:**

_____

_____

_____

Start Date: _____

Finish Line Date: _____

EVENT:

FINISH LINE

Be ALERT Near the Finish Line

As we near the Finish Line, I leave you with a final set of thoughts about climbing to new heights of professional success and bringing in new revenue.

Always be aware of the world around you—the world that competes for your time, energy, resources, and revenue. Sales professionals get pulled in so many different directions that distractions can easily knock them off the track and into the hands of defeat.

The best overall strategy for winning on the sales field is to be aware of opportunities, threats, strengths, and weaknesses. The sales race is competitive, yet if you are aware of the pertinent issues, you will find fewer hurdles and a straighter track.

Use the *BE ALERT* formula to keep your eyes from wandering.

■ B = Benefits

Always help your clients focus on your product's benefits. Remember that you must use the "What's in it for me?" approach. The sooner you understand that clients purchase benefits associated with a product or service, rather than purchasing features, you will experience a drastic increase in sales.

Make a list and keep it handy so that you are always prepared to present the proper benefit for a given situation.

■ E = Enthusiasm

Selling is about excitement. As you sell, you should notice the clients body language and voice inflection. Your client should be excited about buying from you. If he or she is not, then take a look in the mirror – perhaps your lack of enthusiasm is preventing you from making more sales.

■ A = Aware of Opportunity

Great sales professionals are always looking for the next opportunity. They read newspapers and trade publications, ask for referrals, and anticipate client's problems and concerns in order to offer solutions. In a way, sales professionals are like detectives, they search for clues to discover new sales.

■ L = Listen to Needs

When you are with a client, please remember to ask open-ended, thought-provoking questions. Urge the client to talk about both old and new issues. As you listen and respond to the client's replies, try to cover pertinent topics and obtain information for future opportunities. When you listen carefully and actively, the wealth of information you hear is invaluable.

■ E = Evolve New Ideas

Again, it is important to act as both a detective and a problem solver for your client. Seek new opportunities and find new uses and potential customers for your product or service.

■ R = Referrals and Relationships

If you only learn one thing from this book, this should be it: More than 90 percent of sales professionals forget to ask for a referral, which is unfathomable when you consider that it is the easiest thing to ask of a client.

Can you image never having to make another cold call again? Can you imagine getting a majority, if not all, of your business from referrals? It is easy to do. The next time you sell something, simply say: "Thank you for your business. It is people like you that truly appreciate the value of my services. Do you know of someone else who can use this? I am looking to grow my business with more satisfied customers like you."

■ T = Timing and Trends

Selling is about hard work and timing. The tragic events of September 11th set off a lot of long-term economic volatility. Sales dropped, companies of all sizes suffered the negative effects of that horrific day, and there was nothing that any sales professionals could do about it. The only thing that you can do in such a business climate is simply ride out the storm and hope that the economy will bounce back sooner rather than later.

We must BE ALERT to our existing customers. We must provide excellent service so that we do not succumb to competitive threats.

Finish Line selling is uncompromising. We must remain focused, enthusiastic and knowledgeable, and we must always BE ALERT. Selling is fun; selling is difficult; selling is challenging; and selling is about crossing the Finish Line!

Write down 10 Winning Ideas from this book:

1. _____

2. _____

3. _____

4. _____

5. _____

6. _____

7. _____

8. _____

9. _____

10. _____

Write down three ideas that you plan to implement as a result of this book:

1. _____

2. _____

3. _____

When will you get to the Starting Line? _____

Name your Coach: _____

> *"So long as new ideas are created,*
> *sales will continue to reach new highs."*
>
> —Dorthea Brande

Part 5:

In the Locker Room

■ *Suggested Resources from Coach Drew*

The following annotated resources are here to provide you with tools for life long learning. A track is a continuous circle and so is learning. Education in the sales professional is a daily must.

Books

■ Barron, Renee (1998). *What Type am I.* New York, New York: Penguin.

This is a wonderful book that assists you with personality assessment. This book will help you learn more about your and help you build rapport with clients.

■ Blanchard, Ken & Bowles Sheldon, (2001). *High Five.* New York, New York: William Morrow and Company, Inc.

Once again Ken Blanchard knows how to motivate the individual for his or her best performance. High Five provides wonderful techniques and principles to help take your selling to a new level.

■ Blanchard, Ken (1993). *Raving Fans.* New York, New York: William Morrow and Company, Inc.

This Blanchard work is yet a classic to help you build creative alliances with your customers and prospective clients. Use the techniques and watch your relationships be better for it.

■ Carlson, Ph.D., Richard (1997). *Don't Sweat the Small Stuff.* New York, New York: Hyperion.

Riding the sales roller coaster gets obscene. Dr. Carlson illustrates how to smooth out the issues of the day and let you focus on important issues not trivial.

■ Carnegie, Dale (1936). *How to Win Friends and Influence People.* New York, New York: Pocket Books.

Anyone worth their title and business card must read this perennial classic from the selling master. In fact anything Carnegie should be the mantra for most selling professionals. Read Carnegie and you will be better for it. Read this book and learn more about you and relationships than you ever imagined.

■ Carnegie, Dale (1944). *How to Stop Worrying and Start Living*. New York, New York: Pocket Books.

Another classic from Carnegie and a great one at that! This work illustrates how to compartmentalize the most difficult calls and issues to make a better day and a better life.

■ Godin, Seth (2003). *Purple Cow*. New York, New York: Penguin.

Targeted more for the marketing professional, this book includes useful techniques for a selling professional. One of the best is "Be remarkable"—leave a lasting impression for higher levels of sales and service.

■ Hill, Napoleon (1960). *Think and Grow Rich*. New York, New York: Fawcett Crest.

A classic motivational book, written by Napoleon Hill and inspired by Andrew Carnegie, it was published in 1937 at the end of the Great Depression. The text is founded on Hill's earlier work, The Law of Success, the result of 25 years of research based on Hill's close association with a large number of individuals who managed to achieve great wealth during the course of their lifetimes. This is a must read for the spirited selling professional wanting to achieve new levels of success!

■ Mandino, Og (1968). *The Greatest Salesman in the World*. Hollywood, Florida: Fell Publishing Company.

The Greatest Salesman in the World is a classic guide to the philosophy of salesmanship. A parable set in the time just prior to Christianity, the book illustrates the 10 principles for selling success. Written more as an inspirational story the book might confuse due to implication but definitely worth the read.

■ Mandino, Og (1975). *The Greatest Miracle in the World*. Hollywood, Florida: Fell Publishing Company.

This is another classic by Mandino. The ending is a surprise and yet very motivational. If you are seeking a great pick-me-up, this is the one!

■ Parinello, Anthony (1994). *Selling to Vito*. Holbrook Massachusetts: Adams Media Corporation.

Looking for a new method to get into see the decision maker, this is the book for you. Good techniques and advice.

■ Peale, Norman Vincent (1956). *The Power of Positive Thinking*. New York, New York: Fawcett Crest.

The widest read self-help book of all time. You will get positive motivation from this book and you will view the world differently when you conclude. This is a must for the lone selling professional that frequently gets down on him or herself.

■ Robbins, Anthony (1991). *Awaken the Giant Within*. New York, New York: Summit Books.

Awaken the Giant Within covers a wide range of topics, from goal setting, to Neuro-linguistic programming (NLP), personal finance, and relationships. A large book and not a classic but adapts well to Generations X and Y.

■ Whiting, Percy (1947). The Five Great Rules of Selling. New York, New York: McGraw Hill Book Company.

A classic book on selling, this is the book that got Dale Carnegie and Associates started. The book contains a formula for those just beginning selling as well as a great review for the advanced representative. This is a must read for all groups and one that you must have in your library for easy reference.

■ Ziglar, Zig (1985). Secrets of Closing the Sale. New York, New York: Berkley.

Similar to Dale Carnegie, Zig Ziglar is a master of selling success and a wonderful individual. Zig illustrates through the art of persuasion how to effectively thwart objections to close sales quickly.

Audio Products

■ Tracy, Brian (2002). *The Psychology of Selling*. Minneapolis, Minnesota: Nightengale-Conant.

Brian Tracy lays a 12-point goal-achieving method for reaching whatever destination you choose in life, how to "program" yourself for success, which products are best for you to sell, how to "read" your prospect's needs, and how to overcome objections, and how to motivate 99 out of 100 potential customers to buy. He is a bit monotone but most people investing in the profession listen to Brian.

■ Tracy, Brian (2002). *The Psychology of Success*. Minneapolis, Minnesota: Nightengale-Conant.

Recorded similarly to The Psychology of Selling, provides a 12 point blueprint for peak performance and high achievement. The recording is also very monotone yet offers great goal setting techniques for those that want to be high achievers.

Newspapers and Magazines

■ The Wall Street Journal

200 Burnett Road, Chicopee, MA 01020
(800) 568-7625

In order to know your client and your prospective customers you must remain in line with the news and ahead of the competition. *The Wall Street Journal* is the premier source of business, industry and financial information. Make this a part of your daily reading. An online subscription is also available.

■ The New York Times

229 West 43rd Street, New York, NY 10036
(800) 698-4637

As a former East Coaster this is one of my favorite reads for its insightful articles and research of industries and the world. This daily periodical provides excellent current event and business infomraiotn. An online subscription is also available.

■ Personal Selling Power

www.sellingpower.com

Selling Power is read by all sales and marketing professionals that require education and seek monthly advise to expand their business and techniques. Articles are current and trendy and assist professionals from the beginner to the advance selling practitioner. Monthly articles are also written with the entrepreneur in mind. Definitely worth the investment.

Websites

■ www.reuters.com
Reuters is the oldest information provider of financial and business information. The resources are incredible so that you can remain current on business and industry news with capabilities of delivering content directly to your email account.

■ www.factiva.com
Factiva®, from Dow Jones, provides essential business news and information together with the content delivery tools and services that enable professionals to make better decisions faster. Factiva's unrivaled collection of more than 10,000 authoritative sources includes the exclusive combination of The Wall Street Journal, the Financial Times™, Dow Jones and Reuters newswires and the Associated Press, as well as Reuters Fundamentals, and D&B company profiles. Executives, information professionals, marketers, salespeople, and other professionals can easily monitor and understand the latest news, market trends, and business challenges relevant to them—directly from the Microsoft® Office and job-specific applications they use every day. This is a subscription based service but one you must have to assist your selling efforts!

Associations

■ Toastmasters International
PO Box 9052
Mission Viejo, CA 92690
(949) 858-8255

Toastmasters offers a proven way to improve your communication skills. By participating in a fun and supportive Toastmasters group, you'll become a better speaker and leader and gain confidence to succeed in whatever path you've chosen in life. This is a great venue if you fear making presentations to one or more people. Toastmasters will build your confidence.

■ National Association of Sales Professionals
8300 N Hayden Road, Ste 207
Scottsdale, AZ 85258
(877) 800-7192

The National Association of Sales Professionals (NASP) officially started in 1991, although meetings date back to the early 1980's in Chicago. Michael

Reagan was the founder and remains member 001 and participates in the organization's activities. The organization was founded on the princliples that Sales needed a group to certify, organize, and develop people. The organization has over 5,500 corporate and individual members, all of whom are leaders in their respective fields. Great opportunities for networking.

■ Sales & Marketing Executives International, Inc.

P.O. Box 1390
Sumas, WA 98295-1390

SMEI is the premiere international organization dedicated to providing a forum for knowledge, growth, leadership and connections for the community of sales and marketing professionals. Founded in 1935, with over 10,000 members around the world. SME is a good association for both education and networking.

■ Acknowledgements

A work such as this comes not only from the heart and mind but from a team of people that are helpful supportive and loving. No team operates from one heart.

I am deeply indebted to Elaine Floyd for her painstaking and thorough criticisms of this book. In many cases she invested more time and critique than I did the book. Elaine my editor, my publisher, my friend, this endeavor would never be complete without your perfection and acute senses. In addition, many thanks go to Doug Peters for his creativity, his vision and his spontaneity of taking a blank screen into beauty.

Linda Henman, thank you for your guidance and your wisdom and helping me to find ways to work smarter not harder. And thank you to my teacher and best critique, Alan Weiss, Ph.D. who has taught me the art of perfection, and persistence.

To all my friends, at Inscape Publishing that helped supply materials to help me understand personality. And to all my clients former and future, thank you for your support, your friendship and your teaching.

To Dale Carnegie, though we never met, your words, your teachings, your passion have instilled in me a path and purpose I never dreamt possible.

I wish to thank Anthony "Box" James my mentor and my friend, who took me from obscurity and developed me into a man of purpose. God rest your kind soul!

For Gloria and George Jeffrey, my angels and guiding light, I will never forget you and your love helps me to reach new heights each day.

Christine, my soul mate, my love, thank you for your patience and listening to me ramble and for and for Andrew and Ashley, daddy loves you so much, yes I am finally walking away from the laptop!!

■ About the Author

Drew Stevens knows how to get you results! He is a career sales and customer service professional with over 25 years of experience. His consulting firm, Getting to the Finish Line, has attracted clients such American International Group, Hilton Hotels, AT&T, The Federal Reserve Bank, Reliv International, The New York Times, Mercy Health Plans Quicken Loans and over 500 other leading organizations.

Drew serves on the boards of directors of eMed International and St. Louis chapters of Meeting Professional International and American Society of Training and Development. He holds the designation of Certified Sales Professional with the National Association of Selling Professionals and founding member of the St. Louis Sales Professionals Association.

His speaking and consulting enables him to travel over 50 days per year to clients and conferences around the globe. In the last several years Drew has provided advice to well over 60,000 selling professionals. Drew is an adjunct instructor with several universities in the St. Louis area teaching graduate students in the field of entrepreneurialism and international business marketing and strategy. He is an instructor with Webster University and Maryville University's Graduate School of Business and holds frequent marketing and selling seminars with Webster University's Center for Professional Development. He holds a Ph.D. in Organization and Management with an emphasis in personnel development and work performance.

Drew's prolific publishing includes over 150 articles on sales and selling strategy and four books including *Split Second Selling, Spilt Second Customer Service* and *Little Book of Hope*. Some of his works appear in Chinese and Hindi.

He is interviewed and quoted frequently in the media, with prestigious periodicals such as *Personal Selling Power* and *Sales and Marketing Management*. Drew's career has taken him around the globe to places such as Singapore, Johannesburg, South Africa and New York City.

Drew lives in St. Louis, Missouri, with his wonderful wife and soul mate Christine and his two children Ashley and Andrew, (affectionately known as "I Want" and "Get Me").

Index

My accomplishments are:		Rating My Skills *from 1 – 9 (1 being the lowest)*	Prioritize where I need assistance now!
P	Preparation		
R	Rapport		
A	Attention		
C	Convincing		
T	Time Management		
I	Interest		
C	Close		
E	Evaluation		

My accomplishments are:		Rating My Skills *from 1 – 9 (1 being the lowest)*	Prioritize where I need assistance now!
P	Preparation		
R	Rapport		
A	Attention		
C	Convincing		
T	Time Management		
I	Interest		
C	Close		
E	Evaluation		

SALES PLANNING GUIDE

The following questions and statements will assist you in trying to a game plan and a path to selling to new and existing accounts.

Account Name: _____ Date: _____

Primary Contact: _____ Title: _____

Type of Business: _____

Objective of the Call: _____

_____

What are my prospects goals? _____

_____

How can I help my prospect? _____

_____

What information must I know about my prospect?

_____

_____

_____

INFLUENCERS	**RECOMMENDERS**
Name: _____	Name: _____
Title: _____	Title: _____
Name: _____	Name: _____
Title: _____	Title: _____
Name: _____	Name: _____
Title: _____	Title: _____

SALES PLANNING GUIDE

Perceived Needs of the Prospective Client:

PERSONAL	**BUSINESS**
1. _____	1. _____
2. _____	2. _____
3. _____	3. _____
4. _____	4. _____

Needs and Benefits that I need to develop

1. _____

2. _____

3. _____

4. _____

Questions to ask to assist in developing the needs.

1. _____

2. _____

3. _____

4. _____

My Company's Strengths and Features that need to be mentioned.

1. _____

2. _____

3. _____

4. _____

Anticipated Objections and Responses:

	OBJECTIONS		**RESPONSES**
1.	_____	1.	_____
2.	_____	2.	_____
3.	_____	3.	_____
4.	_____	4.	_____
5.	_____	5.	_____
6.	_____	6.	_____

Features and Benefits:

	FEATURES		**BENEFITS**
1.	_____	1.	_____
2.	_____	2.	_____
3.	_____	3.	_____
4.	_____	4.	_____
5.	_____	5.	_____
6.	_____	6.	_____

What are the next steps for this account?

_____

_____

_____

SALES PLANNING GUIDE

The following questions and statements will assist you in trying to a game plan and a path to selling to new and existing accounts.

Account Name: _____ Date: _____

Primary Contact: _____ Title: _____

Type of Business: _____

Objective of the Call: _____

_____

What are my prospects goals? _____

_____

How can I help my prospect? _____

_____

What information must I know about my prospect?

_____

_____

_____

INFLUENCERS	RECOMMENDERS
Name:	Name:
Title:	Title:
Name:	Name:
Title:	Title:
Name:	Name:
Title:	Title:

SALES PLANNING GUIDE

Perceived Needs of the Prospective Client:

PERSONAL	**BUSINESS**
1. _____	1. _____
2. _____	2. _____
3. _____	3. _____
4. _____	4. _____

Needs and Benefits that I need to develop

1. _____
2. _____
3. _____
4. _____

Questions to ask to assist in developing the needs.

1. _____
2. _____
3. _____
4. _____

My Company's Strengths and Features that need to be mentioned.

1. _____
2. _____
3. _____
4. _____

Anticipated Objections and Responses:

OBJECTIONS	**RESPONSES**
1. _____	1. _____
2. _____	2. _____
3. _____	3. _____
4. _____	4. _____
5. _____	5. _____
6. _____	6. _____

Features and Benefits:

FEATURES	**BENEFITS**
1. _____	1. _____
2. _____	2. _____
3. _____	3. _____
4. _____	4. _____
5. _____	5. _____
6. _____	6. _____

What are the next steps for this account?

_____

_____

_____

Feature	Bridges	Benefit

Feature	Bridges	Benefit

Feature	Bridges	Benefit

EVIDENCE	FEATURE	BRIDGE	BENEFIT

E	Example	
A	Analogy	
G	Graphs	
E	Exhibits	
R	Referral	
T	Testimonial	
R	Real Stories	
E	Evidence	
A	Annual Report	
T	True Statement	
S	Statistics	

Goals

- **S**: _____
- **M**: _____
- **A**: _____
- **R**: _____
- **T**: _____

Athletes: Identify things/people to help your reach your goals:	*Spectators*: Identify things/people that hold you back from reaching your goals:
_____	_____
_____	_____
_____	_____
_____	_____
_____	_____
_____	_____

Habit Identifier

MY BAD HABITS	**IDEAS THAT INSPIRE RESULTS**
_____	_____
_____	_____
_____	_____
_____	_____
_____	_____
_____	_____
_____	_____
_____	_____
_____	_____
_____	_____
_____	_____
_____	_____
_____	_____
_____	_____

Keep in mind that it takes 21 days to make or change a habit.

1	2	3	4	5
6	7	8	9	10
11	12	13	14	15
16	17	18	19	20
21				

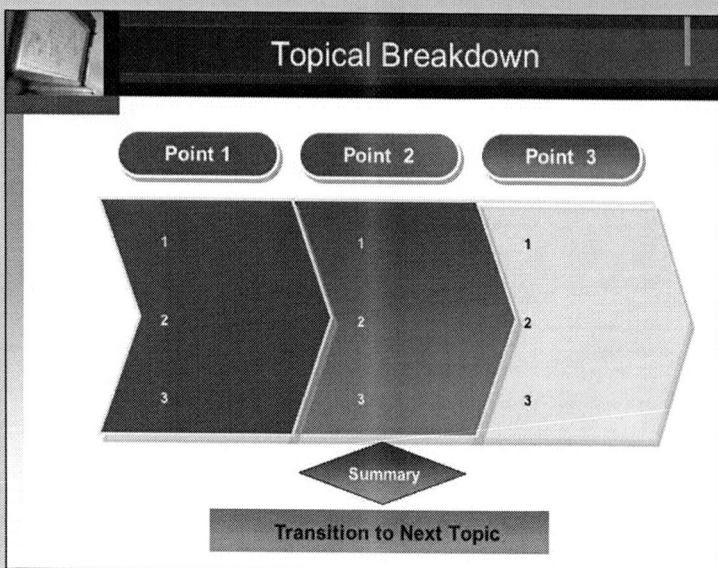

Topical Breakdown

Point 1 | Point 2 | Point 3

1 2 3 | 1 2 3 | 1 2 3

Summary

Transition to Next Topic

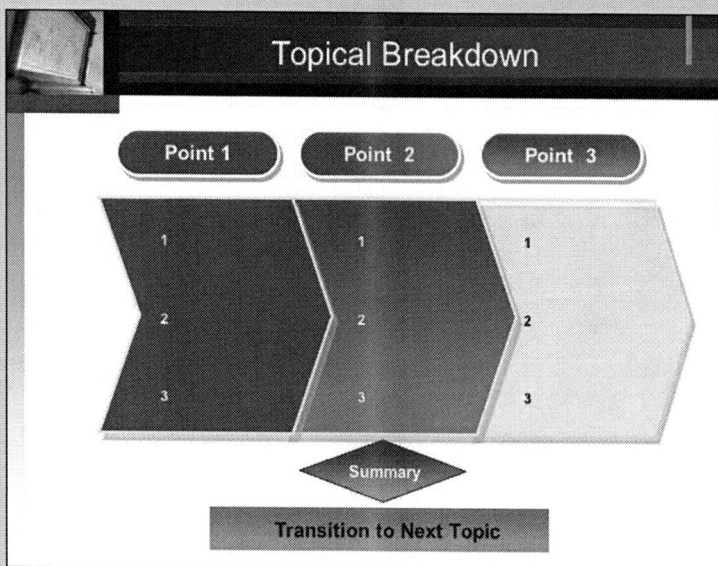

Topical Breakdown

Point 1 | Point 2 | Point 3

1 2 3 | 1 2 3 | 1 2 3

Summary

Transition to Next Topic

REASON FOR MOVING FORWARD	IDEAS AGAINST
_____	_____
_____	_____
_____	_____
_____	_____
_____	_____
_____	_____
_____	_____

NEGOTIATION PLANNER

General Objective _____

Philosophy _____

Issue _____

Strategy	Yours/Theirs
_____	_____
Strengths	Weaknesses
_____	_____
Opportunities	Threats
_____	_____

Tactics _____

Questions	Objections
_____	_____
Evidence	Alternatives
_____	_____

Position Type _____

Opening Offer	Best Offer
_____	_____
Worst Offer	Walk Away Offer
_____	_____

241

REASON FOR MOVING FORWARD	IDEAS AGAINST
_____	_____
_____	_____
_____	_____
_____	_____
_____	_____
_____	_____
_____	_____

Negotiation Planner

General Objective _____

Philosophy _____

Issue _____

Strategy	Yours/Theirs
_____	_____
Strengths	Weaknesses
_____	_____
Opportunities	Threats
_____	_____

Tactics _____

Questions	Objections
_____	_____
Evidence	Alternatives
_____	_____

Position Type _____

Opening Offer	Best Offer
_____	_____
Worst Offer	Walk Away Offer
_____	_____

PRACTICE Split Second Selling Every Day in Your Territory

If you want to obtain single versions of the following forms for your continued use, please email, Info@gettingtothefinishline.com and place in the subject line: Split Second Forms.

If you seek further methods to help you gain Split Second Results every day, purchase *Split Second Selling The Field Guide* and receive $10.00 off as a buyer of *Split Second Selling*.

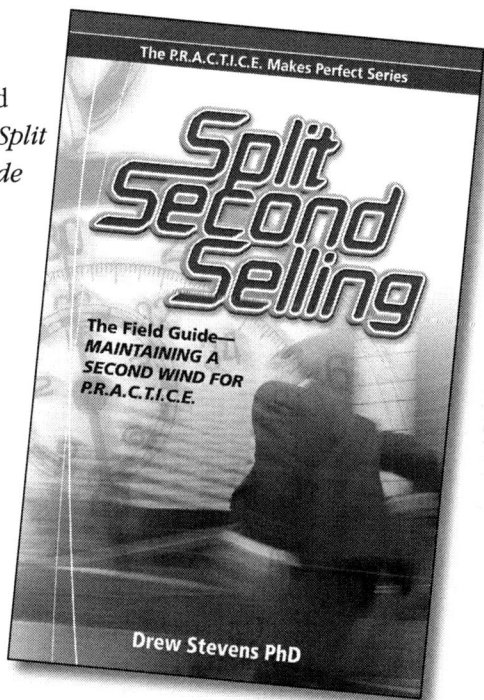

Visit:

www.gettingtothefinishline.com/products

Getting to the Finish Line Products

Audios and Books

_____	*Split Second Selling* (paperback)	$24.95
_____	*Split Second Selling* (hardcover)	$29.95
_____	*Split Second Selling* Field Guide	$19.95
_____	*Split Second Customer Service*	$24.95
_____	*The Little Book of Hope*	$9.95
_____	Finish Line Sales Manual	$149.95
_____	Finish Line Selling Audio Program	$349.95
_____	Magnetic Leadership	$14.95
_____	Winning Time Techniques	$99.95
_____	Leadership Live Seminar	$399.95
_____	Sales and Management Assessments	please call

Please order at *www.gettingtothefinishline.com/products.php*

Or call us at: Getting to the Finish Line, (636) 938-4486

Coming Soon ...

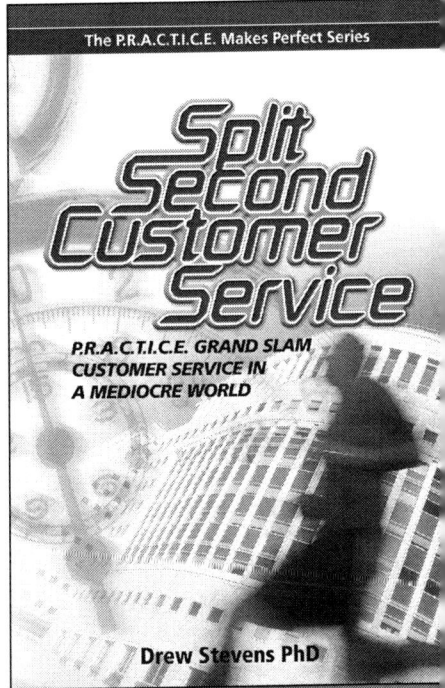

Getting to the Finish Line Products

Audios and Books

_____	*Split Second Selling* (paperback)	$24.95
_____	*Split Second Selling* (hardcover)	$29.95
_____	*Split Second Selling* Field Guide	$19.95
_____	*Split Second Customer Service*	$24.95
_____	*The Little Book of Hope*	$9.95
_____	Finish Line Sales Manual	$149.95
_____	Finish Line Selling Audio Program	$349.95
_____	Magnetic Leadership	$14.95
_____	Winning Time Techniques	$99.95
_____	Leadership Live Seminar	$399.95
_____	Sales and Management Assessments	please call

Please order at *www.gettingtothefinishline.com/products.php*

Or call us at: Getting to the Finish Line, (636) 938-4486

Do you hear any of these statements in your workplace?

☐ Employees don't do what is asked
☐ There is conflict among coworkers
☐ There are arguments with clients
☐ Sales professionals lack focus

Are you seeking relief from:
☐ Decreased teamwork?
☐ Poor client relations?
☐ Decreased profits?
☐ Decreased productivity?

Or do you desire:
☐ Acquisition and retention of talent in a dwindling labor pool
☐ Development of staff from increasing need of productivity
☐ Productivity and morale development in a disloyal work team
☐ Cross cultural consideration of work teams and clients

Getting to the Finish Line clients receive:
☐ Enhanced communication and appreciation of work teams
☐ Creation of selling efficiencies for quicker profits
☐ Lessen hurdles to enhance customer service and lasting client relations

Our services include:
☐ Training and Organizational Consulting
☐ 360 and Behavioral Assessments
☐ Executive Counseling
☐ Facilitation and Training

If you have issues with the above call 877-391-6821 or email Drew Stevens at drew@gettingtothefinishline.com to gain immediate results!